P9-AFV-570

The Sign in
Sidney Brustein's Window

The Sign in Sidney Brustein's Window

A DRAMA IN THREE ACTS

by

LORRAINE HANSBERRY

RANDOM HOUSE : NEW YORK

FOR

Robert Nemiroff

AND

Burt D'Lugoff

AND

the committed everywhere

Foreword

In 1959 I dined with Kenneth Tynan at Sardi's on a first night. There wasn't much doubt about the verdict of the reviewers, only about how nasty it would be. There's no point in dancing on the corpse of that particular play; it was, and quite rightly, doomed from the start.

Nevertheless, I couldn't help feeling that what Walter Kerr and the rest had done had no connection whatever with criticism. To produce a coherent and literate review in one hour is an extraordinary feat; as a professional writer, I am honestly dazzled by it. But it is a feat which has about it the atmosphere of the circus sideshow. It's a job which could be performed even more quickly by a computer.

What I fiercely objected to that night at Sardi's, waiting for the papers to arrive, was that the verdict was completely and savagely final. Since the play in question was a bad one, it didn't really matter; the kangaroo court wasn't hanging an innocent man. Sooner or later, however, a good play—perhaps even a great play—would be condemned to death. Of its very nature the kangaroo court must be more often wrong than right.

With Lorraine Hansberry's *The Sign in Sidney Brustein's Window* it seemed to do just that, not with overt condemnation, but with the kind of "mixed notices" which spell death in a theatre where $6.90 buys the cheapest orchestra seat. The verdict was not reversed: there is no recorded instance of a drama critic having admitted himself to be mistaken. But the public can, as in this remarkable instance they did, storm the courtroom and set the prisoner free. The world was the richer for it. For a great play (I shall repeat that—a great play) not only entertains but enriches, not only takes us out of ourselves but into ourselves as, nakedly, we are.

Let me be absolutely honest: I went to see Miss Hansberry's play partly because of *A Raisin in the Sun* and partly because it was the only new Broadway play I could easily obtain a ticket for. I paid for the ticket myself; I didn't know anyone connected with the production, and if the play hadn't held my interest I would have walked out; I won't accept boredom meekly.

There was a moment early on in the play when I became irritated because one wasn't told just where Sidney Brustein gets the money for his apartment in Greenwich Village and what does appear to be a pretty high standard of living. Then I realized that it didn't matter, because Sidney is a real person, as is everyone else in the play. Perhaps he writes Westerns under a pen name or has a private income; such things have been known to happen. It's a curious trait of drama critics that they'll accept the most fantastic variations of sexual behavior as credible but not be willing to accept that a man isn't always prepared to disclose the source of his income.

Apart from this there are no secrets in the play. No secrets but many levels. It is drama of such clarity that one may return to it again and again, and, I expect, emerge as deeply moved—and each time the more illumined. And here, I imagine, we come to the true reason for the drama critics' less than enthusiastic reception: the fact that there are no characters that can be dismissed or defined on the basis of personal relationships alone. Each is larger than expectation has permitted either them or us. There are no merely supporting actors, the equivalents of the spearman and the butler and the maid. All are real. All are involved in the lives of Sidney and Iris Brustein and they are all involved in their own lives. They aren't there simply as sounding boards for Sidney, as sitting ducks for him to knock down, as causes for him to fight for. This isn't the sort of play with the hero (and sometimes the heroine) twopence-colored and the other characters penny-plain. Miss Hansberry, I am convinced, doesn't know how to create a character who isn't twopence-colored, who isn't gloriously diverse, illuminatingly contradictory, heart-breakingly alive.

From casual beginnings, lightly and humorously entered into, the play becomes Sidney Brustein's personal odyssey of discovery, a confrontation with others in the process of which he discovers himself.

His friend Alton, because his skin isn't white, has from his birth lived in a world of injustice; he is a victim, a martyr whether or not he wants to be one. This doesn't, however, prevent him when he discovers the truth about Gloria from being as prejudiced, as narrow, as unthinkingly cruel as the world which has persecuted him. To be a victim does not necessarily improve one's character, to live in a world without love is not the best way of learning how to love. Alton is intelligent and sensitive and warm-hearted, and yet he behaves as badly as a white man would do in the same position; and this is only one of the instances in which Miss Hansberry refuses to be influenced by progressive prejudices—which can be as blind and stupid as reactionary prejudices.

Indeed, she must have shocked a great many people whose pride is that they are unshockable. Mavis, one feels certain, knew in her heart that Goldwater was right, and is not only a segregationist but anti-Semite; but she is also intelligent and gentle and generous and brave and without hate, growing in one marvelous scene under Sidney's very eyes.

And David, the playwright, too is shocking. It's all very well for an audience to be asked to sympathize with a homosexual's sad predicament; it's a different matter when we are shown that they are not only victims but make others their victims, that some do actually corrupt youth, and that above all, homosexuality is not a special order but a form of sex:

> "If somebody insults you—sock 'em in the jaw. If you don't like the sex laws, attack them . . . You wanna get up a petition? I'll sign one . . . *But*, David, please get over the notion that your particular sexuality is something that only the deepest, saddest, the most nobly tortured can know about. It ain't—it's just one kind of sex—that's all. And, in my opinion—the universe turns regardless."

It is all the more shocking when the author shows David's corruption without moralizing and with a strict and terrible compassion. This corruption is Gloria's too; one speaks of her life of shame entirely without irony.

Colored men don't behave badly, homosexuals and prostitutes have the role of victim, and plays about people like Sidney Brustein end either in defeat or, which is the same thing, a retreat into the teddy-bear world of Jimmy Porter.

This was, in the eyes of the critics, the worst offense of all; the play ends on a note of affirmation. Sidney and Iris are going to drag themselves to their feet and keep going forward. There are ways of evading the struggle, but they reject them. Sidney Brustein is a fool:

> "A fool who believes that death is waste and love is sweet and that the earth turns and men change every day and that rivers run and that people wanna be better than they are and that flowers smell good and that I hurt terribly today, and that hurt is desperation and desperation is—energy and energy can move things . . ."

This is the right ending not only for them, but for us, the audience; or so, at least, I felt, walking out into Broadway remembering words I hadn't thought of for years: If you don't like the world, you can change it.

I can only repeat that *The Sign in Sidney Brustein's Window* is a great play. The word "great" is, I know, grotesquely misused, but no other adjective is possible. The New York drama critics, partly because of the crippling limitations under which they work and partly because of the narrowness of their prejudices, didn't recognize the play's greatness. I am convinced that, sooner or later, with one production or another, in this country or another, the public's judgment will prove better.

John Braine

Introduction

The One Hundred and One "Final" Performances
of *Sidney Brustein*

> I care. I care about it all. It takes too much energy *not* to
> care . . . The *why* of why we are here is an intrigue for
> adolescents; the *how* is what must command the living.
> Which is why I have lately become an insurgent again.
> —Lorraine Hansberry

At 8:50 on the morning of Tuesday, January 12, 1965,
Lorraine Hansberry, aged thirty-four, died of cancer. That
same night, in respect to her memory, Henry Miller's Theatre stayed dark. It did not reopen thereafter and *"The Sign
in Sidney Brustein's Window* went into the record books"—
as the *Herald Tribune* reported it—"after an extraordinary
run on Broadway of 101 performances."

At some midpoint in those 101 improbable performances
the press began to call *Sidney Brustein* "one of the most
talked about plays in years," and it certainly was that; but this
is the least of a story that has already become something of
theatrical legend. It is the quality of all legends (even in
realms not nearly so fanciful as the theatre) that they tend
to grow out of all proportion to the facts. But in the case of
Sidney Brustein the facts themselves are impressive enough.
I was present throughout the two years in which the author—
the remarkable, beautiful woman who meant more to me
than any other person in life—battled so valiantly and, to

the end, indomitably, against the foe that finally took her. These were the same two years in which *Sidney Brustein* came to life. And in the last months it was my job, as one of the producers, at each of these 101 performances to share with the audience the day-to-day facts of the struggle to keep it alive. I cannot pretend to objectivity about either the play or its author; I must leave that to time and to others. But the facts are another matter; they should be allowed to speak for themselves. It is thus appropriate to set them down, for they are not unrelated to the quality of the play—and of the life it embodied.

In the weeks just prior to the opening of *The Sign in Sidney Brustein's Window,* Lorraine resided, with a nurse in attendance, at the Hotel Victoria, where she might be close to rehearsals. She did not know the nature of her illness, only that she was terribly sick and that it might be some time before she could work again at full capacity. Nights were the worst—when she would often waken in agony. And she had developed, too, a corollary ailment to her lowered resistance: shingles—a blistering of the skin that girdled her torso with fire. Medication brought some degree of relief and at times she was, in fact, relatively free of pain. In a piece written for *Playbill* years earlier she had described how a friend, a much older woman "who had lived a purposeful and courageous life and who was then dying of cancer, . . . saluted it [this enemy] without despondency, but with a lively, beautiful and quite ribald anger. . . . There was one thing, she felt, which would prove equal to its relentless ravages, and that was the genius of man. Not his mysticism, but man with tubes and slides and the stubborn human notion that the stars are very much within our reach."

It was that way with Lorraine Hansberry. The "beautiful, ribald anger" with which she greeted fate and the humor without which she could never approach any one of her characters, even those she most admired, were not reserved for the stage. Even in the last months, she would often sit up with her dear friend Dorothy Secules, or myself, in some mugging pose or another, with a hot-water bottle perched debonairly atop her head, her lips turned up, and her eyes wide. And then she would collapse with laughter.

Autumn being ever her favorite season—"melancholy autumn," as she always called it—she was able to take in its vistas and watch the leaves turning on "jaunts" about Central Park in a wheel chair. She managed to attend a certain number of rehearsals and previews—most often she would force herself to take a taxi the three blocks to the Longacre Theatre and then walk, for the wheel chair embarrassed her—and she did an amount of writing.

In a Sunday *Times* article written in this period, for the opening, she summed up what she considered to be "the core" of her play:

> Few things are more natural than that the tortures of the *engagé* should attract me thematically. Being 34 years old at this writing means that I am of the generation which grew up in the swirl and dash of the Sartre-Camus debate of the postwar years. The silhouette of the Western intellectual poised in hesitation before the flames of involvement was an accurate symbolism of some of my closest friends, some of whom crossed each other leaping in and out, for instance, of the Communist Party. Others searched, as agonizingly, for some ultimate justification of their lives in the abstractions flowing out of London or Paris. Still others were contorted into seeking a meaningful repudiation of *all* justifications of

xv

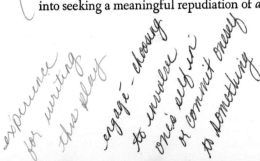

experience for writing this play   engagé - choosing to involve one's self or commit oneself to something

anything and had, accordingly, turned to Zen, action painting or even just Jack Kerouac.

Mine is, after all, the generation that had come to maturity drinking in the forebodings of the Silones, Koestlers and Richard Wrights. It had left us ill-prepared for decisions that had to be made in our own time about Algeria, Birmingham or the Bay of Pigs. By the 1960's few enough American Intellectuals had it within them to be ashamed that their discovery of the "betrayal" of the Cuban Revolution by Castro just happened to coincide with the change of heart of official American government policy. They left it to TV humorists to defend the Agrarian Reform in the end. It is the climate and mood of such intellectuals, if not these particular events, which constitute the core of a play called *The Sign in Sidney Brustein's Window.*

The play opened Thursday, October 15, 1964, to mixed notices, not surprisingly, as I look back on it now. For apart from its human essences and the distinctively irrepressible humor without which Lorraine Hansberry could never approach any character, even those she most admired, *Sidney Brustein* was among other things a "play of ideas"—and thus, from the start, a somewhat alien visitation to Broadway. At best such plays, which have never been entirely at home here, tend to make us nervous, save on the special occasions when they bear the prior stamp of British approval. To make matters worse, it was a play of ideas that are not popular: ideas that ran deliberately counter to the entire vogue of sophisticated *ennui,* the self-absorption, negation, disenchantment and despair that pass for "depth" in the theatre today—again, in those rare instances when "ideas" are admitted at all.

At a critical moment Sidney Brustein, who like so many of

us has transformed the tensions of our age into a personal internal ulcer, is offered the only remedy that seems within his ken: a tranquilizing pill. He reaches out for the pill and, lifting it aloft—as the stage directions say, "like Poor Yorick's skull"—he exclaims: "Yes, by all means hand me the chloroform of my passions; the sweetening of my conscience; the balm of my glands. Oh blessed age! That has provided that I need never live again in the full temper of my rage. . . ." And then, setting it down again on the table, he continues: In another day, Sidney laments, his ancestors might have confronted evil with a sword: "But how does one confront these thousand nameless faceless vapors that are the evil of our time? Could a sword pierce it? . . . Wrath has become a poisoned gastric juice in the intestine. One does not *smite* evil anymore; one holds one's gut, thus—and takes a pill."

In the face of such a world, in which passion has all but lost the name of meaningful action, a world faced at any conceivable moment with extinction beyond the control of any man, it is understandable that the fashion should be despair: that all appears absurdity and that nothing could seem more irrelevant than the quest for alternatives. The very day the play opened Khrushchev fell from power in Russia, the Conservative Party fell in England, and the Chinese set off their atom bomb; where such events can occupy twenty-four hours, what power can a single man feel over the shaping of his destiny? Belief, confidence, hope—commitment of any kind, any act or movement designed to achieve anything at all—the very words become gauche and embarrassing.

And yet it was in the face of just this world, and moreover, with full and unblinking recognition of the *actuality* of the evil within it; and with awareness too, awareness only too personal, of the ultimate absurdity of individual fate, the inevitability of the pain and suffering inherent in the "human condition"—that she set out to *realistically* affirm the species. It was Lorraine Hansberry's stubborn notion that mankind might yet muddle through. Or that, in any event, we deserved the *chance* and that only this was worth the candle.

Distance, however, seems to lend perspective. The goal she set herself, in all her work, was a task possible—or at any rate, easier of achievement—in the crucible of a John Procter, the court of a Hamlet or the Thirty Years' War of a Mother Courage: those moments of man's past when he stood on the brink of a great decision, and heroic action could have clear meaning. It was a task possible even in the slums of Walter Lee Younger's Chicago where black and white are, still more pronounced than our intermediate gray. If the playwright's commitment were less universal, bounded by race or restricted by color, she might have turned for her affirmation, for example, to Mississippi. Instead, she chose to look for it in the most unlikely place of all: the lives most of us lead today. Precisely, in short, where *we* cannot find it. It was the mark of her respect for us all.

The play she wrote was not neat, simple or "well-made" for easy assimilation at one sitting. Rather than essaying a single domestic situation or even several themes, which would ignore the complexity we live with, she deliberately chose to confront the "thousand nameless faceless vapors" of evil that preoccupy and compel us. It was a sprawling canvas on which are juxtaposed, with varying degrees of success, the dominant themes and conflicts which, *only* in their totality and terribly complicated interrelationship, motivate and define our generation. And she did not even allow herself the cover of obscurity. Lorraine Hansberry insisted on clarity *in* complexity. She tackled sacred cows quite as if she did not acknowledge their sanctity, and she had the temerity to discuss ideas *per se* quite as if she did not know she was *not* George Bernard Shaw.

Nor was the play easily classifiable; it could not be comfortably pigeonholed by the first-night critic with a deadline to meet. It was not the exercise in "naturalism" we blithely tend to assume for the social playwright. Neither did it have the familiar tone or attitude that makes more experimental forms acceptable. It was too *popular,* too hopeful, too readily accessible to—and respectful of—the intelligence of the mass audience to be taken for "serious" drama; there was too damn much fun in it. And not one symbol you could not understand. *"There are no squares, Sidney: everybody is his own hipster, believe me when I tell you."* In the simplistic universe of a theatre that has discovered "guilt" and the great new revelation, "original sin," there is something obviously disconcerting—and therefore "sentimental"—about a 34-year-old author who can, after properly nailing the "bourgeois Philistine" that is Mavis Parodus, proceed to turn right around and pay her tribute—and, moreover, actually raise fists to the gods in her behalf, as Sidney does. There is something almost indecent about this; it is an unforgivable lapse, the final fall from sophistication. For it smacks of the suggestion that there is perhaps a potential in her (and if in Mavis, why not in us all?) greater than environment has permitted. And didn't this go "out" with the thirties, at least among "serious" men?

Finally—the cardinal sin—*Sidney Brustein* mixed *styles!* For all the oft-remarked-upon felicity of the playwright's dialogue, her wonderful ear for the comic nuance of every-day, it flows freely—as William Gibson observed in the Sunday *Times*—in a "range of vibrant rhetoric new in her work and not common on our stage." And it also takes flight into a heightened poetic compression permissible in Ionesco and Beckett but not in popular drama—as in Act III, Scene 1, where the disintegration of Sidney's world is paralleled in a disintegration of realistic form.

This stylistic unorthodoxy created certain problems—and ultimate failings—in the production. On stage we tend to consider it enough to *suggest* intellectuals; but too much talk, the actual discussion of ideas, makes us nervous. Heightened speech in an otherwise realistic and comprehensible play, shifts of style, flights of metaphor—are likely to embarrass the actor. The obvious solution is to cut them. And all the more so when we accept the notion, as most of us in the theatre seem to, that there is some inherent, God-given or natural law governing the precise length a play may be— quite as if the fifteen minutes more or less were dictated by some immutable, pre-tested Audience Attention Span Meter, rather than by Stagehands' Union Local #1, and the commuter timetables of the New York Central.

Psychological factors alone are not insurmountable, but when they are combined with the practical problems of production,* there is seldom time for ideal solutions. Something had to give; and the production on opening night suffered

---

* In the case of *Sidney Brustein,* the replacement of our original male star and director two weeks before the opening by Gabriel Dell and Peter Kass, respectively. Mr. Dell's last-minute approach to the role of Sidney— who never once leaves the stage—was the achievement of a fine actor and, in the pitifully short time available to him, the excitement and insight with which Mr. Kass infused the entire company were little short of incredible.

somewhat from both too much cutting and too little. In a few instances themes and character developments arose without adequate grounding in what went before: in Act I, Scene 1, Sidney's crucial decision—which gives shape and direction to everything that follows—was not sufficiently established; and, most notably, identification with Iris, his wife, was diminished by the omission of Act II, Scene 1. The present edition corrects these omissions—and also includes certain minor additions from the author's original drafts that are interesting in themselves.

Looking back to opening night it is hardly likely, in short, that the critic comfortably settling back with nostalgic reminiscences of *A Raisin in the Sun* could have been prepared for *Sidney Brustein*. Only five years before, at the curtain of what is by now one of the best-loved plays in America, the Younger family had decided to risk all for the new home in the white middle-class neighborhood; now their creator was saying that that house was on fire, the community a disaster area of the soul, and that a great deal of rebuilding would have to be done from the ground up if the neighborhood was to be fit for the Youngers to live in at all. And she was saying it in terms—a style, a frame of reference, a genre—quite different from those the critic might have expected of her.

The fact that all of this was implicit in *Raisin* itself—which was actually no more "naturalistic" than its successor; and which did *not* have a "happy ending," only the commitment to new levels of struggle—did not help. For this had quite managed to escape most of the critics at the time, and has eluded them ever since, in the quite understandable rush of their enthusiasm for the new playwright's humor and insight, and the near-ecstatic discovery that she had *not*, praise

God, written a play "about Negroes but human beings." As if, apparently, there were some inherent contradiction. (Imagine, if you can, the suggestion that "Tennessee Williams does not write about Americans, he writes about human beings.")

Closer examination might have revealed, of course, the deeper non-naturalistic levels of *Raisin*. Walter Lee Younger's "African" soliloquy, for example, is a speech that could not possibly *literally* be his own—any more than Mavis Parodus could, in life, become Medea, or Gloria so eloquently locate her essence in a Goya etching. The liquor that loosens Walter Lee's tongue releases a language and imagery he could *not* have derived from the books he has never read, nor certainly from the movies that he *has* seen; and language is *not* a quality of the blood. It is the *potential* talking in him, not the actual. It is the stature to which he aspires, not the one he has been permitted. The chauffeur becomes one with African kings—and in poetry's swift illumination we are enabled to grasp, in full pathos, the extent of the disparity: the size of the injustice that has been done him. The moment has nothing whatever to do with naturalism, literalism or "kitchen-sink" drama. It can only be understood as poetic compression, larger than life. (Just as in the Act II curtain the yardstick in Sidney's hand becomes, visibly, the measure of his— and our own—diminishment.)

A closer look might have revealed, too, the philosophical current that is as strong in the Younger living room as in the Brustein's—if less obvious where the idiom is folk, not Freud; and the allusions are to Tennessee, not Paris.

MAMA
. . . Child, when do you think is the time to love somebody the most . . . it's when he's at his lowest and can't believe in

hisself 'cause the world done whipped him so. When you starts measuring a man, measure him right, child, measure him right. Make sure you done taken into account what hills and valleys he come through before he got to wherever he is.

Is there any essential difference—except for the language—between Wally O'Hara in Act III and *this* about Asugai, the African revolutionist in *Raisin:*

WALTER

You and that boy that was here today. You all want everybody to carry a flag and a spear and sing some marching songs, huh? You wanna spend your life looking into things and trying to find the right and the wrong part, huh? Yeah. You know what's going to happen to that boy someday—he'll find himself sitting in a dungeon, locked in forever—and the takers will have the key! Forget it, baby! There ain't no causes—there ain't nothing but taking in this world, and he who takes most is smartest—and it don't make a damn bit of difference *how*.

Or is Sidney Brustein "that boy" *circa* Greenwich Village in chukka boots and corduroy?

There is a clear line between the plant that sits in Lena Younger's window and the Sign that hangs in Sidney's. But *Raisin* had never received that kind of examination. Perhaps because of its author, perhaps because of its hopefulness, perhaps because of its popularity—we do not associate "serious" art with mass success—it was *assumed* to be simple. The very art by which it concealed its complexity was its critical undoing. Was it likely, then, that the critic, with all the best intentions in the world, was psychologically prepared to accept from the pen of this engaging young Negro writer—"hardly more than a girl," as one interviewer described her—

what he might have from an author of another milieu or more awesome repute?

It was with many of the above things in mind, but also the prayer that I was far wide of the mark, that I worded my opening-night telegram to Lorraine. Paraphrasing freely from the play, it read in part:

> Witness you ever-burning lights above: we fools are up and at it again: fools who believe that death is waste and love is sweet and people want to be better than they are . . . Whatever the outcome tonight I want you to know:
>
> 1) That it is a great play: a measured, remorseless, dimensional paean to life such as no one—no one—has the courage to write these days.
>
> 2) It is a play for people. They come, they laugh, they take sides, they participate; it is their play and it speaks for them—this much is proven already. Let us hope now that the intellectuals surprise us with the depth to rise to their level.
>
> 3) It is not the best production, but it is the very best production we had in us to give.
>
> 4) If the sign hangs long in the window, it is your sign . . . you are tough, Lorraine Hansberry . . . even wracked with pain as now . . . Tougher and stronger and more beautiful than any of us. You are the best that we have. Good health, justice tonight and more to come.

As far as my earlier prayers were concerned, I might as well have saved them for a better purpose. There was justice "to come." But not that night.

Daily reviews are of brief dominion—absolute but without duration. Their hour of ascendance, while it lasts, is awesomely real; their justice swift, final, irrevocable. It was not that the reviews were negative. Far from it. Among them there were a goodly number of outright "raves." But in the main they so utterly failed to comprehend or evoke the play.

Howard Taubman's notice in *The New York Times* focused on "a scene more searing than anything on Broadway," —Alton's monologue—"[which] could stand alone as a passionately eloquent sermon for a time when the Rev. Dr. Martin Luther King also wins a Nobel Prize." He spoke of others "that shine with humor, tremble with feeling and summon up a vision of wisdom and integrity." But he also found that "although the stage frequently lights up, it is likely to dim unexpectedly. The trouble is not only in the writing"—which struck him as uneven and in need of tightening—"one has a feeling that the performance has not quite jelled." Walter Kerr in the *Herald Tribune* largely concurred, and Richard Watts in the *New York Post* shared Taubman's reservations. Yet Watts recognized, too, "a courageous, compassionate and warmly human spirit . . . power and insight and . . . forthright integrity" and, above all, "the unsentimental sympathy for the weaknesses of man" which he felt to be "the notable feature of this searching examination of troubled human nature. *The Sign in Sidney Brustein's Window* demonstrates again that Miss Hansberry is a talented and important dramatist." But in the *Journal-American*, John McClain summed up its essence otherwise: "The theme seems to be . . . 'don't pick on the world.' "

A few reviewers, however, had no difficulty with the theme—or what their colleagues complained of being the multifarious themes—and grasped the play in larger dimension. Publications as diverse as *The Journal of Commerce, New Leader, Saturday Review* and *National Guardian* were unstinting in their respect and admiration. But it remained for the *Wall Street Journal*'s Richard P. Cooke, in a straight "rave," to rejoice: "If Broadway has needed a play by someone who can reach into the turbulence of contemporary life and come up with a true report which is also a work of dramatic art, Lorraine Hansberry has accomplished it. . . . The taste left in the mouth after the final curtain is both bitter and good. For the playwright herself has taste, of the best kind."

Richard Gilman's assessment in *Newsweek*, however, was in direct opposition to Cooke's; it was headlined "Borrowed Bitchery" and is worth quoting at length for the sense it gives of the intensity of emotion the play had succeeded in generating. In coming directly to the point, Mr. Gilman did not waste one word on cast or production:

> There was surely a dry agony in Lorraine Hansberry's writing of *The Sign in Sidney Brustein's Window* . . . the play is a vicious sitting in judgment on others. . . .
>
> There is a sort of inverted miracle in the way Miss Hansberry manages to distort so many things—taste, intelligence, craft. . . . Her dragooned themes . . . serve exclusively as containers for her venomous anger: she hates homosexuals, liberals, abstract artists, nonrealistic playwrights, white people unwilling to commit suicide . . . her savage assault on intellectuality brandishes every intellectual catchword. . . .
>
> . . . In turning into a cocktail-party shrew, in shifting her suffering to the backs of others, in using every easy trick to destroy what threatens her, she has betrayed not only the function of art, but social responsibility, political possibility, her own cause [?] and, most radically, herself.

In his defense of civilization, Richard Gilman was not alone. Others might lack his articulateness, but Martin Gottfried, for one, of *Women's Wear Daily,* was not lacking for courage: he used a bold phrase, the "stinking triviality of it all." Michael Smith, in the *Village Voice,* explained how he "loathed" being forced "to condemn Miss Hansberry's play" and how at first, in fact, he had intended to pay her the tribute of silence: "I would prefer not to cause her further pain. But the play is dreadful, and I am deeply offended at the praise it has received for reasons that are certainly questionable"—the foremost being, he found, "that Lorraine Hansberry, the play's author, is a Negro"—and the next, "the public knowledge of [her] critical illness."

Such comments, however, were the exception. Most reviewers praised the play or its parts in varying degree and combination. But there were strong reservations, too, and an all-too-apparent perplexity about the whole. Where *Raisin* was "warm, simple and direct," *Brustein* was apparently "depressing, diffuse and confusing . . . too many stories . . . too much talk." McClain—who was perhaps typical and who had left in the end "rejoicing"—concluded on a plaintive note: "As I say, I was finally won over—I really came to care —but I wish Miss Hansberry hadn't talked quite so much." A Newark colleague wished she "could have said something *simpler.*"

By merely *cataloguing* what she did say—the themes out of the context of flesh and blood; the ideas isolated from the emotions of those who hold them on stage; the problems apart from the complexities out of which they arose; the characters defined only by their most readily apparent aspect—the reviews, even many of the favorable ones, had made *Sidney Brustein* seem *impossible:* a lifeless tract, a potpourri of "wailings and woes." It was like reporting George Bernard Shaw —everything but the humor. A straight-faced inventory of the characters in *You Can't Take It with You*—or a synopsis of *Hamlet*—would have been about as persuasive.

In the light of such reviews the lay theatre-goer might logically assume modest success—and indeed, many of our friends called to offer congratulations. But to anyone who understands the stringent economics of Broadway the contrary was clear. The play was not a "smash." It was not a musical or a comedy and it had no great star. There had been no great advance sale, and no line would form at the box office next morning. There would be no calls from the brokers and theatre-party agents who provide the lifeblood of Broadway but cannot afford to take chances: the next sale depends on the largest number of satisfied purchasers of the last. Furthermore, the play would have no appeal to a not inconsiderable portion of the public: those for whom it does not matter so much *what* they see as long as they can say it was a "hit." And those for whom this is *all* that matters: a pair of "hot tickets" is but the means to an end, a form of currency, not art—or even "entertainment," except as an item for tax deduction. Without these a play cannot run: the drama that is not a "hit" is dead. *Sidney Brustein* cost $20,000 a week just to operate. *It would have to close.*

Serious theatre-lovers who had read the reviews were intrigued, of course, and many certainly planned to see it sooner or later, but that was beside the point: at $7.50 a throw (plus dinner and baby sitter?) to see for oneself is an indulgence; how many of us can afford the luxury of having our own taste? The only way to evaluate a critic is to match him against the play he reviews. Make the comparison often enough, and one begins to get the feel of the man; only then can one know whom, if anyone, to rely upon. But who can afford it? Instead, we are forced to rely on the internal logic of the review itself. If the man writes well enough, we are likely to be persuaded. And if we are persuaded often enough, he becomes a great critic. But how *well* he writes may have nothing whatever to do with the plays he reviews. It is a perfect closed circle (which is perhaps why it is *known* as the Critics' Circle).

It is only in this context that the New York critic has assumed a power he never sought (and not infrequently protests against—to deaf ears): he is one of the few men with the power to both deliver a verdict—and get rid of the evidence. As Viveca Lindfors was to put it presently: "At the post-mortem there is almost never a corpse." Unless, in short, a large transfusion of money were immediately available, the Sign in our window would have to come down Saturday night. All this was apparent 2 A.M Thursday when, with wondering eyes, we heard the reviews on the phone.

On Friday we broke the news to Lorraine. She had half expected it. As one who knew the ways of this world only too well, Lorraine Hansberry was always more surprised by success or good news of any kind than the contrary—and thus able to enjoy it the more. Her own earlier triumph; the proper recognition of anyone else's achievement; the plaudits of the tastemakers for work of any kind that was genuinely good—these, to her, were always happy accidents, to be treasured to the full, but never counted on. "*A lot of people 'have it' and they just get trampled to death by the mob trying to get up the same mountain*"—if there was one thing Lorraine Hansberry did *not* believe, it was that talent will "out" in the end.

Still, it was the *immediacy* of the prospect that hurt. *Sidney Brustein* had shared the history common to most plays: the years in the writing, planning, production; the lonely vigils, endless drafts, conferences, crises, battles, debates, casting calls; sessions with actors, directors, designers, up to and down through the rehearsals themselves. *A Raisin in the Sun* had run nineteen months on Broadway. Now to run *not even one week*—can any writer be *prepared* for this?

Some scenes one does not ever forget: Lorraine's always deep, penetrating eyes wide with concern as we talked—what if it were a long time before she could write again? What would she do? How would she live? . . . And in the midst of this, a phone call from Frank and Eleanor Perry, the young couple who had written, produced and directed the film *David and Lisa*. Three days before, they had lent the production $2,500 to be used *only* if the reviews were good and we ran. Now, despite the odds, they were saying: "Yes, we've read the reviews . . . no, we don't give a damn . . . we know the odds . . . we're calling to say we hope you will use it. . . ."

Twenty-five hundred dollars, though, was like a drop in the bucket, even when supplemented by a like amount from a friend, Victor Rabinowitz, who said he also knew the odds, but would leave the discretion to us. The next day was Saturday, the day for which the closing notice had already been posted. My co-producers (Burt D'Lugoff and J. I. Jahre) and I spent the night on the phones. Trying, as someone said, to "hold back the ocean."

About noon Saturday Lorraine called from the hotel—one of the few occasions I can recall terror in her voice. The numbness, which since yesterday morning she had felt in her legs, had gradually moved up to her chest. If she did not know the full significance of this, we did: cancer had invaded the central nervous system. Burt D'Lugoff, my partner and for many years our dear friend, who shares the dedication of this book, is a doctor. He told Lorraine he would be right over. I stayed on the phones while he and a nurse took her to the hospital for what was to be the last time.

A member of the production called, a by-now familiar voice though we had only met at rehearsals, who at her own insistence must remain anonymous. She had been thinking, she said: over many years she had been associated with many shows, but never one like this . . . "that *mattered* so much . . . it should not be *permitted* to close." She had $8,500 in the bank, would that help? This was not a woman of wealth (though of good earning power), and so I said no, or started to—she would not even hear me out. How dare I say no? It wasn't *my* play . . . in short, she *insisted*. By now we were both laughing and crying at the same time. This was a Mavis Parodus come to life on the other end of the phone. And as *tough*. I thanked her—wanting to lift my own hands to the gods like Sidney—and got Lorraine on the phone.

"It was like penicillin," Burt later described it, "a radiance, a great beaming smile settled over her face when she heard." For one week at least the Sign would continue to hang in our window. And sometime the next day, alone in her hospital room, she wrote of the play to a friend, in a letter which was never completed. It read in part:

> . . . Yes, a great deal has happened to me since our friendship. In fact, I often feel that everything in the world which can happen has happened to me. But this is nonsense, as a new thing crops up immediately.
>
> . . . I hope that you and Polly get in to see the show. It's

ever so much more entertaining than the reviewers try to let on. *And it's very funny.*

The letter stopped there and these were, so far as I know, the last words she put to paper. Characteristically. For it had never ceased to amaze and delight her that the show really *was* so funny—that people could laugh so loud over the lines —just as it never failed to tickle her that these figments of merest fancy, these characters dreamed up out of her own head, could become real to so many; that people could beam and cry, argue and passionately take sides over them—directors storm and fuss and grow furious, actors create whole past histories and inutterably complicated motivations for them and ask the most intricate intimate questions about them; and that, for instance, there never was an audience that did not burst into howls and applause over Mavis' lines about "squares and hipsters" just as they did over Lena Younger's "*It* expresses me!" Lorraine Hansberry was, among other things, a willful little girl playing a prank, as she sometimes said, on a much too sober and pontifical adult world—and never more delighted than to be caught in the act. It was her *funny* lines—the ones that gave people pleasure—of which she was proudest.

In the next week three people came backstage who were to prove instrumental in keeping the Sign in our window: Sidney Kingsley, Shelley Winters and Viveca Lindfors.

The celebrated playwright had come to see Gabriel Dell, whom he had originally discovered and directed as one of the "Dead End Kids" in his perhaps most famous drama. The word he used most frequently in discussing the play afterward, privately and publicly, was "genius"; he made no secret of the fact there were moments he would have treated differently, but overall he had seen nothing to equal its power and beauty in many years. He was outspoken publicly, and behind the scenes worked quietly and effectively in a dozen ways.

Shelley Winters was at once so moved and so profoundly struck by the play's contemporary relevance—"it is not a play *about* our time," she said at a Presidential election rally, "it *is* our time"—that she offered to step into a supporting role at union minimum if this would help. In the weeks to come, Miss Winters, one artist who has never shunned the *responsibility* of public prominence, was to leave no stone unturned in the play's behalf, appearing again and again, in alternation with Miss Lindfors, on radio, television and the public platform, often on a moment's notice.

The Swedish-born star—surely one of the world's most beautiful women and no less an actress and human being—is proudly American now in all respects except one: she still has some difficulty in accepting the dollar as a standard of art. Viveca Lindfors showed up at our office the following morning in a great fur coat and dungarees and at once proceeded to call and write (typing the letters herself until all hours) others in the theatrical community for support. In the months following, I do not recall her ever declining any request for aid, no matter what the hour or inconvenience. The immediate result of her efforts was a meeting scheduled for the following Friday, after showtime, at the Perrys' home.

On the morning of Tuesday, October 20th, Lorraine Hansberry first lost her sight, then went into convulsions: the disease had entered her brain. At midafternoon she lapsed into coma and the doctors informed us it was now only a matter of hours at best. We released the news for the first time that she was critically ill; there was no longer any point in holding it back. My brother stepped in to take my place in the 'round-the-clock battle of the phones at the office. But she was tough—it is not rhetoric to speak of Lorraine Hansberry's commitment to life; even then, out of the depth of whatever will survived in the darkness that enveloped her, how she clung to it!

Can a person in coma register the world outside? Not once but many times in the next four days I repeated to her the words of a letter from a stranger whom I was later to meet, a young theatre-goer named Howard Bennett, that had arrived at the Longacre that morning. It read in part:

> . . . I would like to thank you for writing *Sidney Brustein*. You have written a beautiful—a painfully beautiful work of art. Please, if *Sidney* fails, please keep writing . . . I don't know why or how it missed being received as one of the modern theatre's greatest achievements. . . .
>
> For my own part, let me tell you that I felt everything that was happening on stage yesterday . . . I believed in everyone, and I hurt—and I saw the beauty in each. Thank you! I hope you will be able to keep carrying a message of hope till the last day of your life. With *Sidney* you helped and touched me as I do not expect to be moved again in the theatre.

Again and again I told Lorraine she would *have* to get better, come back, write again, that there were too many people like this depending on her. Later, when I asked her whether she had heard, she said yes—though I am still not certain of it and do not suppose it really matters now.

Wednesday night we had visitors: William Gibson, whose musical adaptation of *Golden Boy* had opened the night before, and his wife, Margaret. Bill had met Lorraine only on several occasions over the years, yet there was a warm affection between them—she respected his *Miracle Worker,* and she often remarked on one particularly helpful suggestion he had made when *Raisin* was trying out in New Haven. That night was the first opportunity the Gibsons had had to see the new play and they came back to the hospital, late in the night, and he stood for a long time, this tall and somewhat Lincolnesque man, crying by her bed. Afterward, a letter appeared in the Sunday *Times* which, in addition to hailing the play, posed a more general question:

> To the Editor:
> It is one of the vexing facts of our theatre that as audience we have so little sense of its cultural continuity.
> At this writing a play by Lorraine Hansberry . . . is struggling to keep open at the Longacre quite as though Miss Hansberry had never in her life written a line to interest anyone. How can it be that, of the hundreds of thousands who roared with pleasure and wept tears at her *Raisin in the Sun,* so few have the intellectual appetancy to hear what her mind has been at work on since? . . .
> . . . Is it a compliment to our culture that one season a writer can be voted best playwright of the year, and another season be ignored like a novice?
>
> William Gibson
>
> Stockbridge, Mass.

By Thursday the doctors gave up predicting: Lorraine Hansberry had quite confounded their charts. And then, beginning on Friday, she returned gradually to life—slowly at first, unable to speak, hardly able to move, but then growing a bit stronger each day, as first sight returned and partial movement, then comprehension and speech, until finally—

weeks later—she could eat a little again and converse and even be helped out of bed to sit up in a chair. There remained some partial loss of memory, and *aphasia:* the mind functioning clearly but not always able to deliver the right words. But in her last months Lorraine was able to follow with considerable relish the events occurring outside.

At the Friday night meeting at the Perrys' on October 23rd, I was thus able to announce a turn for the better—and from that point on no further reference was made to the matter of her health in the course of our campaign. For if the play were worth saving, it had to be saved on its own account and not that of its author—and indeed, most of those who became involved afterward did not know of her condition, or else assumed she was recuperating, since the malignant nature of her illness had never been revealed.

The most lasting impression that night was not made by any of the theatre folk present. These tended to varying degrees of pessimism—not about the play but about the state of our theatre and the resultant implausibility of the effort: it had been tried and failed too many times before; we might eke out a few weeks at most, but "you can't buck the gods of the box-office . . . give up while you're ahead—or else why not try to move the thing off-Broadway?" The off-Broadway "alternative," which Lillian Hellman had put forward earlier and which Shelley Winters echoed, is without doubt the most frequent one heard whenever a serious play is in trouble, reflecting as it does the despair most of our serious artists feel about survival on Broadway. But it also tends to be defeatist and divisive, since on examination it proves to be not an *alternative* at all: the move is *not possible,* and never has been, for a dozen practical reasons, not the least of which are the union requirements (which will not be waived) for a six months' lapse before any play can be reopened off-Broadway—at less than Broadway salaries, that is.

It was easier, too, to go off on tangents, to discuss, with delightfully interlarded anecdotes, all manner of related aspects—publicity, columnists, etc.—constructive in themselves but beside the immediate point: survival. It remained for a tall young Negro in overalls, who had seen his *first* play not one year before, to set a different tone for us all.

Louisiana-born Jerome Smith is a CORE field organizer who, at twenty-five, had been jailed, beaten and run out of more towns, from one end of the South to the other, than even the theatrical mind can comfortably imagine. He had come to this meeting because he happened to be in New York at the time and because he knew Lorraine and had seen her play. He spoke softly and haltingly now of the particular relationship between them, and the room fell silent: "Two years ago, I first met Lorraine Hansberry—like many of the young people of the movement, I had come to enlist her support." In a few meetings, he said, she had become one of the "important influences in my life, opening up for me books of all kinds"—and ideas that went beyond the particular parochialisms of the immediate struggle. She had helped to organize a great public meeting in Croton-on-Hudson, New York, which she chaired and at which he spoke. The funds collected there had purchased the station-wagon in which the three civil rights workers, Michael Schwerner, Andrew Goodman and James Chaney, were driving at the time of their abduction and murder. Then, with a groping eloquence new to many in the room, Jerome Smith spoke of a "commitment beyond race . . . the need to reach out and touch each other . . . without which civil rights in themselves don't mean a thing"—and it was *this,* he said, which spoke to him through this play about a Jewish intellectual in Greenwich Village "as through few other experiences in my life." There was silence for a moment, and after that the discussion was brief, sober and to the point.

The following week's *New York Times* carried an ad, signed and paid for by most of those in the room. Titled "An Open Letter: First-Rate Theatre Belongs on Broadway," it read in part:

> The news that Lorraine Hansberry's *The Sign in Sidney Brustein's Window* faces closing should disturb all who love the theatre.
>
> Miss Hansberry's new play is a work of distinction. It contains the humor and insight we associate with the finest traditions of our stage, and it is written with profound respect for the human condition.
>
> *The Sign in Sidney Brustein's Window* is concerned with the turbulent life of our times. It is, in turn, powerful, tender, moving and hilarious.
>
> Whether it survives or closes will be determined this week. . . . We the undersigned, who believe in it enough to pay for this ad, urge you to see it *now.*

The signatories of this first ad were James Baldwin, Paddy Chayefsky, Sammy Davis, Ossie Davis, Ruby Dee, William Gibson, E. Y. Harburg, Julie Harris, Lillian Hellman, Sidney Kingsley, Viveca Lindfors, Frank and Eleanor Perry, Arthur Penn and Shelley Winters. They were joined in subsequent similar ads by Alan Alda, Steve Allen, Kaye Ballard, Anne Bancroft, Theodore Bikel, Marlon Brando, Mel Brooks, Frank Corsaro, Tamara Daykarhanova, Keir Dullea, Arthur Godfrey, June Havoc, Lucille Lortel, Bill Manhoff,

Claudia McNeil, Kay Medford, Mike Nichols, Patrick O'Neal, Robert Preston, Lloyd Richards, Diana Sands, Herman Shumlin, Kim Stanley, Joseph Stein, Charles Strouse, George Tabori and Teresa Wright.

Meanwhile things began to happen quite independently of our efforts—and, as a matter of fact, from this point on we were never able to catch up. The play was finding its own voice, generating its own appeal, and the response was rather like the bursting of a dam.

The very day that first ad was going to press we received a call from Blaine Thompson, the advertising agency. Another producer, one of the most distinguished in the business, with a track record running back a generation and with *The Deputy* currently on the boards, had seen the play and, without any knowledge of our ad, had written one of his own which he wanted to pay for and run—if that was all right with us. (It was.)

A FINE PLAY! A MOVING PLAY! A POWERFUL PLAY is on the stage of the Longacre Theatre . . . it is maybe even a great play. It is sharply witty, beautifully acted and brilliantly illuminated by the author's close touch with today, with now. In these days when "to care" is the verb that must govern us, such a play is an exciting, enjoyable experience.

HERMAN SHUMLIN

P.S. I would have been proud to produce it myself.

Other noteworthy ads in the weeks that followed carried a note from Steve Allen:

THIS WONDERFUL, WARM, FUNNY PLAY made me laugh and cry and whistle and stomp. It should run for years. *It must!*

See it! It's the kind of tough, gutsy yet tender drama that the theatre needs.

And there was one ad excerpted from a radio broadcast which merged Arthur Godfrey's great personal enthusiasm with his account of an audience which "just went wild with applause and enthusiasm; people were crying Bravos all over the place. If we can just get [the play] through these holidays, then I think it will settle down to a long run—and well it should."

Wednesday, November 4th, was a most unusual matinee, with some fifty ministers and rabbis—invited by Reverend Donald Harrington, of the Community Church, and Reverend Eugene Callendar, Moderator of the Presbytery of New York—in attendance. "At the final curtain," as one paper reported it, "the mystified audience was invited to remain . . . and share in one of those rare moments in theatre when actors don their street clothes, sit before the proscenium and talk with the people out front." The cast was joined by Sidney Kingsley, Herman Shumlin, Shelley Winters, Viveca Lindfors and James Baldwin. Mr. Shumlin spoke of the "six men" (critics) who require that a play be perfect: "We must change whatever it is in our social fabric which makes the production of thoughtful plays, serious plays, difficult." He pointed to periods in history when, he said, the theatre was emptied of everything but farces, and then theatre died: "What is needed is the realization that there will be no musicals, no farces, if there are no serious plays. There will be no theatre."

The others on stage delivered what were to us, by now, familiar appreciations of the play. And then, one by one, ministers and rabbis arose to discuss its impact upon and meaning for them. Rev. John Garcia Gensel of Advent Lutheran Church had been to see *Brustein* three times—and was planning to come yet again. That afternoon he had brought his sixteen-year-old daughter: "If I am to preach about life—if she is to *learn* about life, about the evil, the corruption, the fallibility with which she will have to contend—then let it be in *this* context!" Rev. Howard Moody, of Greenwich Village's Judson Memorial Church, called the play a "more moving portrayal of deep moral and spiritual problems than all the mawkish sentimentality of our religious dramas—and far too many of our sermons." But it was the son of a Baptist minister, once "called" as a preacher himself, but long since departed from the faith, who touched the spiritual essence of that meeting.

James Baldwin had cut short his work on a movie scenario on the West Coast in response to our appeal. He arrived late, clambered up over the footlights, and standing there, a short, slight figure in chukka-boots, described, with the frankness for which he is famous, his own *negative* reaction to the play on first reading an early draft, and his "troubling ambivalence" after seeing it—". . . until, that is, I realized just what about it was making me so uncomfortable." He continued: "It was the particular quality of commitment in this play. Sidney Brustein believes things that I, that most of us, believed a long time ago . . . in the thirties . . . only Sidney still believes them. And now the poor bastard is a set-up to have his head busted in for it—in the third act he would *have* to. . . . I was *shocked*—and believe me"—he smiled and his eyes crinkled in a great grin—"I am *one* individual I really thought was almost *beyond* shocking—at my own discomfiture . . . at the degree we have, all of us, permitted ourselves to retreat from what we once were . . . at the distance one decade, the era of McCarthy, has driven between us and our own ability to commit ourselves as Sidney is committed." This play was an experience, he concluded, "that caused me to examine more deeply into myself and my own motives than any other in a long, long time. If it cannot survive, then we are in trouble . . . because it is about nothing less than our responsibility to ourselves and to each other."

Out of this meeting came a statement drawn and signed by the clergy in attendance:

> *The Sign in Sidney Brustein's Window* presents almost too poignantly the whole range of the dilemmas and confusion of contemporary man. If it does not contain the answer it presents the challenge. Organized religion cannot ignore this cry for help as well as hope, and it will have to respond with more than a reiteration of time-worn platitudes. . . .

The statement thanked the author for her "humane, wise and deeply perceptive challenge" and on subsequent weekends *Sidney Brustein* was the subject of not a few sermons.

It now became possible to introduce certain of Lorraine's revisions which there had not been time to incorporate prior to the opening. These were not so extensive as has since been supposed. They involved about ten minutes at most—a cut of three pages of quite extraneous dialogue at the very beginning, which I had foolishly resisted earlier; some minor cuts; and the transposition into Act I of a speech from the omitted Act II, Scene 1, which clarified Iris' character. But they did tighten and speed the action somewhat, and on this basis we invited the critics back for a second viewing, and one of them actually availed himself of the opportunity.

Norman Nadel of the *New York World Telegram and Sun* had written by far the most negative of the original daily reviews. It was headlined " 'THE SIGN' IS MUCH TOO SORDID" and had concluded: "I think an audience is willing to forgive most on-stage sin—and in this play it ranges from plain and fancy lying through plain and fancy illicit sex, including voyeurism. But when the sin becomes oppressive . . . it cancels out caring for the people involved. This play sinks under its own sordid substance."

The new review took a quite different tone and in the light of the original is worth quoting at length:

> Nothing in this world remains the same, with the possible exception of faith, nowhere is this better illustrated than in the living theatre. For evidence, turn to the creation, metamorphosis and rebirth of Lorraine Hansberry's new play. . . .

After filling in the background to the new changes, Mr. Nadel said he was "glad" to report that "the play has discovered its own eloquence":

> The first act . . . is [now] a spirited, and even quite tender exposition of a troubled, though not entirely hopeless marriage. . . . Before, it sweated social consciousness. Now, the shrewdly worded truths come forth with far less conspicuous labor. The new spontaneity and conciseness of that first act are worth their weight in gold . . . which could mean box-office gold as the word gets around.
>
> And the improvement in the first act is most significant; it tends to clarify and coordinate all that follows. . . .
>
> Gabriel Dell as Brustein, Rita Moreno as his wife, Alice Ghostley as the suburban sister, and all the cast have enriched and enlivened their roles.
>
> I wasn't alone in my reaction last night. The audience embraced this play, laughed at it, and understood why

everyone on stage felt and behaved as he did. The changes are working, and the play has found its voice.

Perhaps it was the tightening to which Mr. Nadel referred. Perhaps it was the greater security the actors had achieved in an additional two weeks on stage. Perhaps it was a different frame of mind or—as I believe—the greater perspective a second viewing allowed. But, in any event, in the long annals of the daily review, a reassessment of this kind is almost unique.

One rainy Sunday I received a message from the answering service that "a Mr. John Brynn" had left a number. "John Brynn" turned out to be *the* John *Braine,* the celebrated British novelist, who was passing through town on a lecture tour and had happened into the play the night before. Late that Sunday night we talked into the early hours at Downey's. The author of *A Room at the Top* had known nothing of the play, our battle, or indeed its author (other than that she had written *A Raisin in the Sun*), only that it was one of the few plays for which you could buy a Saturday-night ticket. For a "long dreadful moment at the end of the play," as he said, he had feared that she was "giving in" and would come up with no more than the despair that is the fashion in England almost as much as in our own country. "But no—she had gone out facing the guns" as he had hoped she would. His reactions were published as a personal communication in the *Village Voice.* They comprise the foreword to this volume.

The events which in rapid succession followed my meeting with Braine were initiated at a midnight session at the home

of Anne Bancroft and Mel Brooks, which was strikingly—
and sympathetically—reported by the not infrequently acer-
bic Lillian Ross in *The New Yorker*. Titled "Strategy Meeting," her piece began:

> Five beautiful movie and stage actresses, one librettist of
> a current hit musical, one composer of another current hit
> musical, one writer of a new hit comedy, one busy and
> flourishing writer-comedian, and two young producers of an
> economically foundering play got together on a recent Satur-
> day for a midnight meeting to work out some strategy for
> keeping the young producers' play running. . . . They were
> all serious, determined, and ready to fight, and were all con-
> centrating on the play, *The Sign in Sidney Brustein's Win-
> dow*, by Lorraine Hansberry.

Miss Ross quickly revealed that, in addition to Miss Bancroft, the actresses at the meeting were Viveca Lindfors, and
Diana Sands (then appearing in *The Owl and the Pussycat*),
who had first been seen on Broadway as Beneatha in *Raisin*,
and our costars, Rita Moreno and Alice Ghostley.* The li-
brettist was Joseph Stein (*Fiddler on the Roof*), the composer
Charles Strouse (*Golden Boy*), the writer Bill Manhoff
(*The Owl and the Pussycat*), and the writer-comedian Mel
Brooks, our host. The meeting was typical of many in numer-
ous living rooms in the last months of 1964, and out of it
came, among other things, a noteworthy letter by Miss Bancroft and Mr. Brooks—an invitation to a special Sunday
matinee performance for the theatrical community (whose
working members cannot attend other shows on playing

---

* These two, together with Gabriel Dell and our entire cast, were in
fact the unsung heroes of the whole drama, performing not only on stage
but off—yet seldom even knowing for certain whether or not they would
be in or out of a job the next week.

nights). It was addressed "To Our Friends in the Theatre," and was posted on the backstage bulletin boards of all theatres. It opened:

> The show must go on . . . *my show*, baby, not yours!
> This is the selfish truth as we in show business too often have come to know it. But once in a blue moon, a phenomenon occurs. Actors, directors, producers, playwrights, gently lay aside their megalomania and join hands in a common cause. . . .
>
> Last week we saw that play. We had joined the cause originally out of respect for Lorraine Hansberry, but on the way to the theatre we secretly figured it was a bomb. It must be a bomb; Kerr didn't rave, Chapman didn't like it, and Hadassah hadn't bought a single theatre party. Actually we went more out of obligation than anticipation.
>
> We were shocked.
>
> It was a *wonderful* play.
>
> We laughed, we cried, we *thought*. In our opinion . . . *Brustein* . . . is a more mature and compelling work than Miss Hansberry's award-winning *A Raisin in the Sun*.
>
> If there is in you one single filament of curiosity that glows to know what is happening in our theatre today, see it! Now!

The "selfish truth" of which the writers spoke was certainly not in evidence, or in any event predominant, in some circles along Broadway as the year 1964 drew toward a close. In the closing moments of *Sidney Brustein* there is a line to the effect that "people want to be better than they are," and in a small corner of our lives one might have thought the line was coming to life. There is traditionally, of course, a goodly amount of "sentiment" in show business—a performer falls ill for a performance and a dozen stars come forward to leap into his shoes—but this is good for one night, perhaps, and a headline next morning; a movement sustained as this one became can only be understood as the expression of something deeper. Again and again on radio or TV, a star would spend more time talking about the Sign in our window than his own show (half the time we would not even know he was scheduled—the report would filter back later). A Kay Medford would suddenly show up with $100 for an ad, or Teresa Wright would appear and spend days on the phone calling friends "just to see it." June Havoc devoted her entire television show to it one night, and "the Randi Show" turned over five hours on WOR-Radio, from midnight til dawn, to it. The actors in our own company petitioned the union to permit pay cuts and even the traditionally inexorable Shubert Office took a fraction less in rental each week than our contract provided. The cast of *The Subject Was Roses*, with the cooperation of the author, Frank Gilroy, and the producers, started curtain speeches to tell the audience about "the 'other' drama worth seeing in town." And soon Sammy Davis, too, was stopping the applause at the Majestic each night to urge a trip to the Longacre. Other shows—*Any Wednesday, How To Succeed in Business*—stuffed flyers in their programs.

The momentum was not limited to theatre folk. Most significantly, it embraced the audience itself. People would troop backstage every night to ask what could they do, how could they help. Volunteer workers flooded the office, captained by Judy Hankin, Marguerite Kisseloff and Jean Lindgren. Student contingents arrived from outlying colleges and others distributed flyers nightly in Shubert Alley. Larry Butler, a part-time usher and candy-hawker, delivered messages. Mary Ann Mantell, who owns Cædmon Records, taped interviews for radio. Herb Saltzman, marketing director for RKO-General, placed them, and, with Bea Wilson, a public relations expert, and Merle Debuskey, the show's ever-willing but overworked press agent—who had never seen anything like this—concentrated on the mass media generally. Novelist John O. Killens, his wife Grace and members of the Harlem Writers Guild sent out mailings in the thousands.

Charles Belous, Deputy County Attorney of Nassau County, who many years before had been a leader of the La Guardia-Fusion movement, saw in the play a "great new affirmation" of independent, reform city politics and circularized former leaders of the party—Newbold Morris, Charles McGoldrick—for support. Three hundred women met with Viveca Lindfors in Wantagh, Long Island, to consider "the crisis on Broadway" and to garner support. A nursery school director in Great Neck personally called and channelled some four hundred souls to the box office. People called friends. Friends called other friends. And at least one party—Bell Telephone—showed a profit on the show.

A minister at one after-curtain discussion summed it up: this was "*living* theatre, as significant as anything occurring on stage . . . for audiences were reaching out of—beyond—their own lives to become *involved* again, committed, engaged to something larger . . . which can only make us all the larger for it." Irish audiences at the Abbey Theatre in another era might show their passion by rioting; here involvement took another, far less dramatic form, but in its own small way it was no less real.

For all this momentum, however, we still were not out of the woods. The Sign hung, but precariously. Each week attendance continued to grow—not overwhelmingly, but appreciably—and on one matinee day I remember rushing over to the theatre to see a line actually formed halfway down the block. Thanksgiving climaxed our best week yet: we actually broke even. But ahead lay the economic "deep freeze" that comes before Christmas, traditionally the theatre's worst time of the year. These are the doldrum days given over to Christmas shopping and close budgeting in anticipation of the big splurge to come; the nights when all along Broadway you get the feeling that nine million New Yorkers blithely got up that morning and decided, in concert, "Tonight I am *not* going to a show!" Attendance at all shows plummets, and only the big ones—those sold out well in advance by mail and theatre party, or cushioned with a substantial reserve—can survive.

It was with these things in mind, weighing the facts and deciding, for once, to be "realistic," that we agreed we would finally have to close. Unless somehow an additional five to ten thousand dollars could be scared up in loans to meet our anticipated deficit—by now we had run out of names to call and a frantic week on the phones had not turned up any new ones—Sunday matinee, November 29th, would bring down the curtain.

Only—because we had gone so far already that there was nothing to lose—we would "go down fighting." That last performance would be followed by a public "open hearing"—right in the theatre. A telegram, drafted at 4 A.M. at the Brooks' home and signed by 28 of those who had sponsored our ads, was dispatched to Governor Rockefeller, Mayor Wagner, Senator Javits and Kennedy, and Roger L. Stevens, head of the President's Commission on the Arts:

Undersigned urgently request your attendance next Sunday, Longacre Theatre, open hearing re: *Sidney Brustein* and crisis in our theatre.

After endless talk, theatre community now beginning to act. We can no longer permit our finest plays to die. Have joined hands to save a play. We are making it our focus because what threatens it threatens the heart of American Theatre. If plays of such quality, humor, wisdom cannot survive in nation's cultural center, then all of us must seriously question our future in theatre.

Today only 27 shows running on Broadway. Only five dramas—and of these, three have posted closing notices. If theatre continues to shrink, what happens to New York business, hotels, restaurants, trade? What else draws millions here?

It is time cultural and governmental leaders joined forces on behalf American theatre as they have other vital issues. . . . Your presence and participation will underline for all the crucial importance of maintaining first-rate theatre.

The "crisis" to which this telegram referred was in no sense an exaggeration. The three dramas that closed that weekend were *The Physicists* by Friedrich Duerrenmatt, one of the giants of the modern stage, after successive triumphs throughout Europe and in England (three weeks on Broadway); *Poor Bitos* by Jean Anouilh, a great success in London (three weeks on Broadway); and Rolf Hochhuth's *The Deputy*, the only one of the three to enjoy a substantial (though not entirely financially successful) run. *Sidney Brustein* was to be number four—leaving only *The Subject Was Roses* which, with "rave" reviews, a tenacious effort, a cast of three and an exceedingly low break-even point, had managed to last. (The following week *Slow Dance on the Killing*

1

Ground, by William Hanley, opened to raves; it survived for 88 performances.)

That Sunday morning I awoke, for the first time that I can recall in all the weeks before or after, with the *physical* feeling of defeat in the pit of my stomach. This was really it: we had run out of miracles. We had tried but failed—and to *know* you have tried may distract the mind, but it does not lessen the fact of failure. A telegram that morning from Senator and Mrs. Javits "regretfully" expressed great respect for the play (which they had seen) and admiration for our effort—but they would be unable to attend. Another from Governor Rockefeller wished us success: "I share your concern for the future of the theatre and applaud the initiative the theatre community itself is now taking"—but also declined. A third from Senator Kennedy, which he subsequently permitted us to use as an ad—"I urge all friends of the theatre to come to the aid of this play. I earnestly hope that contributions from them will preserve this play for the public and for us all"—brought the same news of commitment elsewhere. The press, which was by now somewhat bored with the whole affair, generally indicated their disinclination to turn out on a Sunday. Only the artists, the audience and Robert Dowling, the Mayor's cultural emissary, would be present.

Nonetheless, at 5:30, when the curtain came down, Ossie Davis—playwright, actor and always one of the theatre's most public-spirited citizens—stepped forward in the midst of an, as usual, sustained ovation, to open the hearing. He spoke briefly, then introduced me, indicating that the crisis in the theatre was "too general an abstraction: let us first devote a moment to the crisis at hand." What followed is perhaps best described in the report carried the next morning by *Newsday,* one of the few papers present:

> New York—In a highly improbably but dramatically superb performance yesterday, the audience at the Longacre Theatre took to the stage to save the play.
>
> . . . When the final curtain fell yesterday, co-producer Robert Nemiroff . . . [announced] sorrowfully, "You have been present at the final performance of *The Sign in Sidney Brustein's Window* . . . unless something happens this afternoon."

> The theatre buzzed with excitement . . .

> "If there is an individual that has the means to help," Nemiroff said, "we'll take a minute or two . . ." And he waited. No big voice spoke up but someone suggested a collection. Nemiroff hesitated. Another audience voice spoke: ". . . We want to save this thing. We want to give money. Take it . . ." But Davis said no, if not enough was collected, how would it be returned?

Yet the more we onstage said no, that it could not be done, that this was "commercial theatre," where you cannot take up collections, it just isn't *done*—and that it could not help anyway because too much was needed—the more the audience, one person after another standing up in his seat, argued back until, finally, in effect, they had shouted us down and it was agreed that we would accept loans. By now there was bedlam in the house—but this was a "mob scene" unlike any other, as the audience rose from their seats, found their own leaders and literally took charge—formed lines, marched down the aisles *and up onto the stage itself* . . . while Ossie Davis read out the names and amounts and I sat down— some say, collapsed—on the Brustein staircase, looking on for the next hour in bemused, if gratified, wonder. *Newsday* concluded:

> ... A collection desk was set up on stage, in the middle of the set of Sidney Brustein's living room. As the audience filed forward, actress Madeline Sherwood ... shouted from the stage: "This is the most exciting thing I've seen in New York."
>
> After an accountant was found in the audience, tabulation began. It totalled exactly $5,000, with $2,500 being given by one anonymous individual. Nemiroff, standing with his cast, actress Anne Bancroft, and Davis, seemed overcome as he announced the play would continue.

That "anonymous individual" was the Mayor's representative, Mr. Dowling, acting as a private citizen on behalf of his own firm. After this, what?

We tried to express the gratitude and the jubilation we felt in our next ad, and it was even possible now to look at the lighter side:

> WE HAVE TRIED REPEATEDLY TO CLOSE THE SHOW, AND THEY JUST WON'T LET US!
>
> We have tried again and again and again—but every time a Shelley Winters, a Herman Shumlin, an Anne Bancroft, three Pulitzer Prize playwrights, or fifty ministers and rabbis in concert say, "You must be out of your mind—it's a *great* show! You *can't* close it!"
>
> Last Sunday we tried again. We announced this had been the last performance. The audience shouted us down ... [and] raised their own $5,000 to continue the show another week.
>
> There must be something there. Not just that *The Sign in Sidney Brustein's Window* is "important," "the most talked about play of the year," or one of the only two dramas

to survive this season. But that people seem to love this play. . . .

Next Sunday we will try again to close the show. So if you want to be *sure* to see it, you will have to catch it this week. On the other hand, you'll be taking a chance: in this business there are no guarantees—and, who knows, we may *never* succeed in closing it.

As a matter of fact, we now discovered to our amazement that we had entered the charmed circle: the *New York Daily News'* "golden dozen"—*Sidney Brustein* was one of the longest running shows of the year on Broadway! (Look down, ye gods, and weep.)

In this fashion we survived the pre-Christmas lull . . . and staggered forward to the next crisis, which was already prefigured, as described in a column by Dorothy Kilgallen:

The entire company of *The Sign in Sidney Brustein's Window*, still bravely trying to keep the play running, is campaigning to raise another $5,000. An anonymous friend has agreed to donate that amount if only they can match it, and that would mean they could move to another theatre. Box office receipts have been going up, in spite of the usual pre-Christmas slump, but they have to vacate the Longacre Theatre next week, no matter how good business gets—and they have no money to move. . . .

Since late October another show had been booked into the Longacre, its tenure to begin just before the twelve days of Christmas—the best time of the year. The simple act of dismembering and moving a set from one Broadway theatre to another would cost us $7,000, plus a new marquee, new posters, new signs, publicity—but there is no point in further painful detail here. Necessity simply produced a new set of heroes: Mr. and Mrs. Stan Frank, Richard Rodgers, Abe Weisburd, Gardner Cowles, Imre Rosenthal, Alan Jay Lerner. On Tuesday, December 22nd, our Sign hung in a new window.

The curtain rose at Henry Miller's Theatre to a jam-packed house—and came down to a thunderous standing ovation. And two days later, on Christmas Eve, we were able —at last, and publicly—to express some measure of what we had felt and experienced. In appropriately seasonal type our ad was headlined: "AND A MERRY CHRISTMAS TO ALL OUR FRIENDS who have made it a happy Christmas for us." There followed simply a list of names. Many have figured already in the telling of this story. Others I have neglected to mention thus far: Charles Taubman, Art D'Lugoff, Jane Lander, Renée Kaplan, Joel Dein, Albert Maher, Marcia Schlather, Peter Mumford, Lillian Gruber, Abbot Simon, Bev Landau, Mrs. Burton Lane, Stephen Silverman, Cora Weiss, Mr. and Mrs. William vanden Heuvels, Theodora Peck, Ruth Nichols, Fran Bennett, Clarence and Ann Jones, Fran Damon, Maurice Gruber, and still others, whose omission must be forgiven me, in immeasurable ways made our continuance possible.

It was not that the appearance of each new friend could be said to have "saved the show" (although in more than one instance that was precisely the case). It was that without them all—together—*The Sign in Sidney Brustein's Window* could never have persisted. For each, at some crucial moment when spirits were lowest, had come forward to provide whatever spark, or inspiration, or money was needed until another could step into the breach and carry on from there.

Not closing, however, did not mean successfully *running.*
Sidney Brustein, in its first run, was not a financial success—
ever. The balcony and mezzanine might be sold out, as frequently they were now, but on Broadway it is the 500-odd
orchestra seats ($6.90 weekdays, $7.50 weekends) that count
—and it was precisely here that we were the weakest. There
was good reason for this. The brokers, business firms, theatre
party agents, who together account for the bulk of these
seats, cannot, as noted earlier, afford to take chances on anything less than a hit. But to be a "hit" in New York you have
got to *act* like a hit. And to act like a hit you must hold the
price line, make no concessions, advertise freely that you are
a hit (our budget did not even permit us to appear in the
alphabetical listings of some papers, and consequently readers assumed we were closed) and have what it takes to back
up the claim: You have to place your tickets on sale far in
advance—which means *not* having to depend on a maximum
sale in the current week—and *know* that you will *be* there
when the date comes round. To sell a theatre party, for example, you must guarantee the agent's commission on the
promised date (it is still painful to recall how many parties
we had, literally, to *turn down* for just this reason!). And
above all, you have to be *sold out* when somebody calls or
comes to the window—or else why should they bother to buy
in advance? The show that depends on its nightly sale is not
only *not* a hit—it cannot become one.

Also, there was that about our entire effort which, meas-
ured strictly in terms of box-office return, was psychologically
self-defeating. In *The New Yorker* we might be "the talk of
the town"—and indeed, from what I am told, there were not
a few homes that winter in which eyes turned first to the
morning headlines over coffee, and then directly to the the-

atrical page for our latest ad, or adventure. But to be *too* much talked about is not an unmixed blessing. In the theatre as in any other business there is no greater virtue than in a certain amount of safe *non*-distinction. It is the better part of valor to be part of the crowd and there is nothing so reassuring to the buyer as a good *conservative* old-fashioned hit; if he doesn't have the greatest evening in the world, at least it won't be the worst.

To appeal for help from the stage is thus automatically to reduce your *natural* appeal; it may carry you through the week but it could cost you the month. It may generate *intensity* of support but, by the same token, vitiate numbers. It is to sacrifice long-run possibility for short-run necessity. For we do not go to plays as a duty or to help others, but to *enjoy ourselves*. And the bolder the campaign, the more precedents overturned, the more some proclaim the values of a play— the more suspect it must seem to others: not *entertainment* but a "cause," edifying perhaps and "good for the soul"—but who wants to spend a night out on his soul?

Nor is there anything mystifying or especially guarded or secret about this knowledge: all that it takes to act upon it is money. If at any one moment we had had the money— *enough* money to proclaim *Sidney Brustein* a hit and *act* like a hit, to be less newsworthy and more safely, securely, conservative—there is little doubt in my mind, to judge from the nightly response of those who did see the show and kept it running week after week, that in short order *Sidney Brustein* would have become just that.

Whether financial success is the only, or the main, criterion of success is another matter, of course, although more and more in our theatre we have come to act and *think* as if it were.

On Broadway today the simple fact is that the play that does not *make* money is a "failure." Not just a *financial* failure but an unmodified failure—one that requires no further qualification. *Sidney Brustein* played to 80,000 people—more than if it had run two years off-Broadway; more than saw *"Morning Becomes Electra"* or *"The Iceman Cometh"* on Broadway, or *Juno and the Paycock* in Dublin or New York; more perhaps than saw *Hamlet* in Shakespeare's London. But in the parlance of Broadway, not just of accountants —in the minds of serious theatre people and even many artists themselves and in the press—80,000 people do not an audience make. As one reporter lamented, with no irony intended, there was "no public" for the play.

As it was, between 7:45 and 8:30 each night we might do one of the busiest window sales in town—and indeed between those hours on a Saturday night we more than once racked up $3,000—but this very fact was our undoing; it left us totally to the caprice of the elements and the mood of the hour. No one was committed *in advance.* A simple shower or snowstorm could throw us deeper in debt. An extended weekend blizzard could wipe us out—as indeed one finally did.

For Christmas, 1964, I bought Lorraine a necklace of delicate gold and amber; of the kind that in years past would have set off the dark coals of her eyes and—magnificently—the brown richness of her skin. Yet seeing it, she was suddenly distressed: "Do you *really* think so? Oh God, if it could only be true—that I could *wear* it!" But she was too wise to play the game of deception and she often talked now of "something horrible" that she felt was going to happen.

lviii

Lorraine Hansberry was never so enamored of life that she would clutch it at any price. But neither for one moment was she one to let it go gently, or gracefully, or with anything less than protest unremitting. What was happening to her I can only describe as indecent, unjust, infuriatingly beyond reason, knowing even as I write that the very words have no relevance—one cannot expect justice or reason of a universe where these are only glorious concepts the living *impose*— *as Lorraine always insisted.* She would have none of the platitudes that might soften her own strong sense of truth or provide easy cover for others. I spent New Year's Eve by her bed and at midnight toasted a "Happy New Year." She made a face harsh with annoyance, and dismissed this utterly, wanting to know what was "happy" about it? She was *not* reconciled.

On the morning of January 12th, she was, I am told, smiling and talkative and then, at about 8:30, she grew suddenly weaker and lapsed into unconsciousness. Just before 9:00 I received the phone call that Lorraine Hansberry was no more.

After that it might perhaps have been possible—with a new sustained effort—to raise the curtain on her play again, but for the moment the heart had gone out of us. *"That is the first thing . . . to let ourselves feel again. . . . Then tomorrow, we shall make something strong of this sorrow. . . ."*

Five years before, at the turn of the decade, a young and healthy Lorraine Hansberry, who had just been awarded the greatest honor our theatre can bestow, had been asked by *Mademoiselle* magazine what she wished for the New Year and the coming decade. She had wished for peace in the world; for plenty for all the people of these United States; for an end to racism; and "a new spirit . . . in the ranks of Negro Leadership. . . ." Her article had concluded with a wish for the arts:

> In the next ten years I hope that serious American art will rediscover the world around it, that our finest painters and writers will dismiss the vogue of unmodified despair in order to pick up the heritage of a nobler art. In spite of some awe-inspiring talents involved in recent writing, the appointment of sinister universality to Ego in settings of timeless torture has been a virtual abdication of the meaning of history, which has been resplendent with what may most certainly be called progress. I hope American creative artists will look again and see that Ego, like everything else, exists in time and context, and that the results of the lives of Abraham Lincoln and Adolf Hitler are hardly comparable, regardless of the common properties of that abstraction, the Ego. Nor is this a call, Heaven forbid, to happy endings or clichés of affirmation. For the supreme test of technical skill and creative imagination is the depth of art it requires to render the infinite varieties of the human spirit—which invariably hangs *between* despair and joy.

Sidney Brustein was that kind of play. The degree to which it succeeded I leave to the reader; but its author was never one to lay down prescriptions she did not herself strive to fulfill. The lines I treasure most from it are the ones which precede this story. They will be inscribed on the author's tombstone in Croton-on-Hudson. They are the essence of her work, her life, and for three months they intruded themselves upon, became part of the lives of a great many others who came to "care," if not "about it all," then at least about something more than they had perhaps permitted themselves to care about for some time.

It wasn't much: for one hundred and one performances we had joined to keep a Sign in a window. But before it came down, *The Sign in Sidney Brustein's Window* had been recognized by thousands for the play it is. As I write that Sign is going up in other windows across the country. And in the years to come it will hang in windows all over the world. But for me, as I suspect for not a few others, it will always hang there at the Longacre Theatre, where, with her own penetrating eyes, Lorraine Hansberry first saw it raised. For there, in spite of ourselves and all our vaunted sophistication, for one brief moment she had helped us each to become— what she always was—"an insurgent again."

Robert Nemiroff
April, 1965

—✳✳✳—

Within a month of its closing, the Sign was hanging again: this second time in a New York suburb, Mineola, Long Island, where in an experimental week—a bold stroke by producer Laurence Feldman—it proved a near sellout. It played to more people than had ever seen it in a week on Broadway. It had engendered requests for production in a dozen countries on five continents and was booked for a Theatre Guild national subscription tour. "It seems incredible that *Sidney Brustein* did not find a large and loving audience in its Broadway run"—wrote *The Los Angeles Times'* Cecil Smith, when the play opened at the Huntington Hartford—"for here is a play so rich and warm and funny and vital and varied, so beautifully written and wondrously performed, that it is worth a carload of slick little Broadway hits."

THE SIGN IN SIDNEY BRUSTEIN'S WINDOW *was first presented by Burt C. D'Lugoff, Robert Nemiroff and J. I. Jahre at the Longacre Theatre, New York City, N.Y., on October 15, 1964, with the following cast:*

SIDNEY BRUSTEIN	Gabriel Dell
ALTON SCALES	Ben Aliza
IRIS PARODUS BRUSTEIN	Rita Moreno
WALLY O'HARA	Frank Schofield
MAX	Dolph Sweet
MAVIS PARODUS BRYSON	Alice Ghostley
DAVID RAGIN	John Alderman
GLORIA PARODUS	Cynthia O'Neal
DETECTIVE	Josip Elic

Directed by Peter Kass
Scenery by Jack Blackman
Lighting by Jules Fisher
Costumes by Fred Voelpel

"The Wally O'Hara Campaign Song" *by* Ernie Sheldon
Production Associate: Alan Heyman
Associate to the Producers: Beverly Landau

The action of the play takes place in the BRUSTEIN apartment and adjoining courtyard, in Greenwich Village, New York City.

Act I

Scene One : Time : This very present. Early evening, the late spring.
Scene Two : Dusk. The following week.

Act II

Scene One : Just before daybreak. The following day.
Scene Two : Evening. Late summer.
Scene Three : Election Night. Early fall.

Act III

Scene One : Several hours later.
Scene Two : Early the next morning.

Act One

SCENE ONE

The setting is Greenwich Village, New York City—the preferred habitat of many who fancy revolt, or at least, detachment from the social order that surrounds us.

At the rear are all the recognizable sight symbols of the great city. They are, however, in the murk of distance and dominated by a proscenium foreground which is made up of jutting façades. These are the representative bits and pieces of architecture which seem almost inevitably to set the character of those communities where the arts and bohemia try to reside in isolation—before the fact of their presence tends to attract those others who wish to be in bohemia if not of it—and whose presence, in turn, paradoxically tends to drive the rents beyond the reach of the former. Tenements of commonplace and unglamorized misery huddle together with cherished relics of the beginning days of a civilization; the priceless and the unworthy leaning indiscriminately together in both arty pretentiousness and genuine picturesque assertiveness.

Thus, here is a renovation of a "Dutch farmhouse"; there, a stable reputed to have housed some early governor's horses; and here the baroque chambers of some famed and eccentric actor. And leading off, one or two narrow and twisty little streets with squared-off panes of glass that do, in midwinter, with their frosted corners, actually succeed in reminding of Dickensian London. The studio apartment of the BRUSTEINS, *at left, is the ground* floor of a converted brownstone, which—like a few other brownstones in the Village—has an old-fashioned, wrought-iron outside staircase arching over a tiny patio where city-type vegetation miraculously and doggedly grows. Beneath the staircase landing is the BRUSTEINS' private entrance. Nearby, downstage right, is a tree.

In the cut-away interior of the apartment the walls are painted, after the current fashion in this district, the starkest white. To arrest the eye—because those who live here think much of such things—the colors which have been set against it are soft yellows and warm browns and, strikingly, touches of orange, vivid sharp orange, and that lovely blue associated with Navajo culture. We can see at once that the people who live here would not, even if they did have a great deal of money—which they certainly do not—spend it on expensive furnishings. They prefer by pocket book and taste—to the point of snobbery, perhaps—to scrounge about the Salvation Army bargain outlets; almost never the "Early American" shops which are largely if not entirely priced for the tourist trade. In any case, a few years ago most things would have been discernably "do-it-yourself" modern in these rooms; but that mood is past now and there is not a single sling chair or low, sharply angled table. "Country things" have come with all their knocked-about air and utilitarian comfort. But there remain, still, crafted ceramic pots of massive rhododendrons in various corners and, everywhere, stacks of last year's magazines and a goodly number of newspapers. The result is that —while it is not a dirty place—clutter amounts almost to a motif. Prints range through reproductions of both the most obscure and the most celebrated art of human history, and these, without exception, are superbly and fittingly framed. And there is a sole expensive item: a well-arranged hi-fidelity

unit, and, therefore, whole walls of long-playing records, and
not one of them at an angle. Fighting them for supremacy
of the walls, however, are hundreds and hundreds of books.
And on one wall—SIDNEY's banjo.

In fine, it is to the eye and spirit an attractive place. Its
carelessness does not make it less so. And, indeed, one might
lounge here more easily than in some other contemporary
rooms—and, perhaps, think more easily. Upstage center is
the bedroom door. To its right, the bathroom. Downstage
left is part of the kitchen area, which disappears offstage.
And, dominating all, upstage left, the large irregularly
shaped bay window, angled out from the building wall in a
skylight effect, in which will presently hang—the Sign in
SIDNEY BRUSTEIN's window.

Time: This very present. Early evening, the late spring.

At rise: SIDNEY BRUSTEIN and ALTON SCALES enter, each
burdened down with armloads, two or three each, of those
wire racks of glasses such as are found in restaurants. They
are heavy and the two men have carried them several blocks.
They are very much out of breath and speak haltingly as
they struggle with the loads. SIDNEY BRUSTEIN is in his late
thirties and inclined to no category of dress whatsoever—
that is to say, unlike his associates, who tend to the toggle-
coated, woven, mustardy, corduroy appearance of the post-
war generation of intellectuals in Europe and America. This
has escaped SIDNEY: he wears white dress shirts as often as
not, usually for some reason or other open at the cuffs—but
not rolled; old college shoes; and whichever pair of trousers
he has happened to put on with whichever jacket he has
happened to reach for that morning; and they will be more
likely mismated suit parts than sports outfits. It is not an

*affectation; he does not care. He is of medium build, vague
carriage, tending to shuffle a bit, except when in a fit of excitement. And his eyes are wider and more childish than the
sort generally associated with the romance of the intellectual.
His sole attractive feature perhaps is a mat of tight willful
dark curls atop his head. He does not wear glasses.* ALTON
SCALES *is a youth of about twenty-seven or so; lithe, dark,
with close-cropped hair. Unlike his friend, he is dressed
in the mustard, corduroy and sweatered manner of his
milieu.*

SIDNEY   Never mind his mother, for Christ's sake. And
never mind the "great swelling crests of water" in his
girl's eyes. Don't bleed it. Write it like you figure we already *care* without you sending up organ music. Follow?
(*He puts down his load and fumbles for his key;*
ALTON *leans against the staircase railing*)

ALTON (*Stiffly*)   I hear what you are saying.

SIDNEY   But *compassion* is consuming your heart and you
want us to *know it*, don't you? The old uptown sob sister
credo: "*In the beginning was the tear.*"
(*He picks up the glasses and they go into the apartment. As the lights come up on the interior,* SIDNEY
deposits his load on the living-room floor)

ALTON   He may die. They said Sal could still die.
(*He racks his glasses up on top of* SIDNEY's *and reels
away with fatigue to the couch, where he drops
down, spent*)

SIDNEY (*Snatches out the page of newspaper copy to which
he has been referring*)   And this is going to save him?

6

He needs *this?* Look, baby, from now on, when we write, let's forget we *absolutely love* mankind. Don't venerate, don't celebrate, don't hallow what you take to be—(*Facing out to the audience with a bit of a smile*)—the human spirit. Keep your conscience to yourself. Readers don't want it—they feel pretty damn sure that they can't afford it. That's why Harvey had to unload the paper. And that's why I am now the proud owner, editor, publisher, guiding light. (*With a flourish, returning the copy to* ALTON) Presume no commitment, disavow all engagement, mock all great expectations. (*His eyes are now only for the audience; scanning our reaction with a wet-lipped savoring*) And above all else, avoid the impulse to correct: all movements, causes, clubs and anti-clubs. It's the only form of compassion left. (*He lights a cigarette and wanders back to the glasses, where he suddenly confronts them with a mock funeral gravity, to the point of making the sign of the cross*) So—there they are: the last remains of the Silver Dagger.

ALTON You're better off. What the hell did you know about running a night club, man?

SIDNEY It wasn't *supposed* to be a night club.

ALTON That's right. It wasn't a night club and it wasn't a coffee house or anything else that anybody ever heard of.

SIDNEY I thought it was something people wanted. A place to listen to good folk music. Without hooked-up come-ons. (*Puzzled, rubbing his face*) I thought there'd be an audience for it. For people like myself. There gotta be people like me somewhere, don't there?

7

ALTON   There are. And they don't go to night spots—of whatever kind—just like you don't.

SIDNEY (*Moving toward the glasses again*)   You know what those glasses really are, Alt? They're a testament to the release of Manny. He's free now, my brother Manny. Free of Sidney. Finally. Let's drink to it. Drink to Manny's absolution.

> (*He crosses downstage left to the counter. It is a combination bar and kitchen surface, on either side of which stand two unfinished wooden stools*)

ALTON   Bourbon for me.

SIDNEY   You can have vodka with ice or vodka without ice. (*Pouring*) Good old absolved Manny. (*Crossing with a glass for* ALTON *and then turning and saluting the racks of glasses once again*) The day he put up the money for the Silver Dagger he sat there with "End of Obligation" written all over him. An expression on his face which read: "This thing will be a failure. But having done this I will have done all I can for Sidney. After that I can call it quits in good conscience. You can do so much and then—well, that's it." So here's to you, Manny, you Prince of Philistines. Sidney the Kook has set you free! To hell with that. (*He puts down his glass, abruptly hauls out a huge pad of tracing paper and a big marking crayon, and sits down at his drawing board, which is framed by the window; it is angled almost horizontally to serve as his desk*) Let's talk about the paper.

> (*With broad strokes he marks off apportionments of space on the sheets*)

ALTON (*Idle curiosity—that is not so idle*) Ahh—Sidney
. . . Does Iris know you've *bought*—and I use the term
loosely—the paper yet?

SIDNEY No.

ALTON Well, don't you think she oughta know?

SIDNEY Yes, I'll tell her.

ALTON When? It's been two weeks already.

SIDNEY (*Trapped, therefore evasively*) When I get a
chance, I'll tell her.

ALTON She's going to have a lot of opinions about it.

SIDNEY She always has opinions. If I paid them any attention I'd never accomplish anything. (*He looks back to his
sheets*) You know what? I think I'd like to try the next
issue in reverse. You know, white on black. What's with
this black on white jazz all the time? People get in ruts.

(IRIS, *his wife, enters with an armful of groceries.
She has not yet reached thirty, is of ordinary pretti-
ness of the sort one does not notice at a distance; but
she is quick with a gamin vivacity that charms utterly
the moment she speaks or one looks in her very large
eyes. And true to a great number of the girls of the
locale, she possesses vast quantities of long, long hair,
presently done up in a French twist. It is dark brown.
Life has already made* IRIS *too nervous and slightly
inclined to hunch. But whatever her accomplish-
ments on stage, she is an actress, given to playful
mimicry, and, at least with* SIDNEY, *she feels free to
play this to the hilt. Between them, though this is*

9

not at all their actual relationship in years, there is more than a little of the adolescent girl showing off for father, seeking his approval, testing the limits of his knowledge and authority; and, especially of late, more than a little chafing at the bonds. He has been her lover, father, universe, god. But the man has feet of clay and, coupled with increasing dissatisfaction with her own state, there is the insistent, though as yet unidentified, need to break free. The tension between them bubbles freely to the surface; yet, save in their sharpest exchanges, there is still the element of banter and fun. At the click of the lock, SIDNEY *thrusts his pad aside. She crosses to the bar, nodding to* ALTON; *stops momentarily at the glasses; throws a look at* SIDNEY; *deposits her groceries; stops again at the glasses; and takes off the raincoat she is wearing to reveal one of those hideous yellow and white uniforms of the kind that are invariably inflicted on counter waitresses in luncheonettes)*

IRIS (*From the glasses to* SIDNEY)   I don't want them in my living room.

SIDNEY   Where else can I put them?

IRIS   We're not going to have the residue of all your failures in the living room.

SIDNEY   Look. Don't start. It's all over. Isn't that enough? (*He crosses to the phonograph and puts a record on*)

ALTON   I just remembered a very pressing engagement someplace.

SIDNEY (*"Don't desert me"*)   Where?

ALTON   I don't know, I'll think of it later.
   (*He exits*)

IRIS   It was all over *before* it started, if you ask me. (SIDNEY
   *does not rise to this; she goes into the kitchen. The music
   comes up. It is a white blues out of the Southland; a lyrical
   lament whose melody probably started somewhere in the
   British Isles more than one century ago and has crossed the
   ocean to be touched by the throb of black folk blues and
   then, finally, by the soul of back-country crackers. It is, in
   a word, old, haunting, American, and infinitely beautiful; and, mingled with the voice of Joan Baez, it is a statement which does not allow embarrassment for its soaring
   and curiously ascendant melancholy.* SIDNEY *busies himself at the drawing board, with an occasional side glance
   toward* IRIS. *The song, "Babe, I'm Gonna Leave You,"
   dominates utterly. Suddenly* IRIS *changes the subject*)
   Ben Asch was in for lunch.

SIDNEY   So?

IRIS   (*Turns off the phonograph*)   He said they're doing a
   tent production of *South Pacific* out on the island this
   summer. Casting now. And guess who's doing it? Harry
   Maxton! Sidney, *Harry Maxton*. Remember, he *loved* me
   when I read for him that time!
      (*She is up and at the mirror whipping through a few
      of the hand gestures which signified "Happy Talk"
      in the original production. Her husband looks up at
      this for a few seconds, sobers, and looks away*)
      "Happy talk, keep talkin' happy talk
      Talk about things you like to do . . ."
   (*Wheeling and facing him exuberantly*)
   Remember—he really flipped for my Liat!

SIDNEY   And he hired somebody else. And you know perfectly well you won't show up for the audition.
(*He is immediately sorry*)

IRIS (*Frozen in the Liat pose*)   You rotten, cruel, sadistic, self-satisfying son of a bitch!
(*She exits into her bedroom*)

SIDNEY   I'm sorry. I don't know why I do that.

IRIS   Then why don't you go find out and give us both a break?
(*He fans that away dispiritedly*)

SIDNEY   Does Steiner really tell you to go around drumming up business for him like that?

IRIS   I have *not* mentioned Dr. Steiner. And I am *not* going to! I am not *ever* going to mention Dr. Steiner in this house again. *Or* my analysis. You don't understand it. You can't—

SIDNEY *and* IRIS (*Together, he wearily with her*)   "Unless you've been through it yourself!"

IRIS (*Re-entering from bedroom. She has changed into tight high-water pants and a sweater*)   That happens to be true!

SIDNEY   Iris, honey, you've been in analysis for two years and the only difference is that before you used to cry all the time and now you *scream* before you cry.

IRIS   *You don't get better overnight, Sidney, but it is helping me!* Do you think that I would have been able to say the things I just said if I weren't going through a *tremendous* change?

SIDNEY (*Genuinely*)   What things?

IRIS   I just called you a sadistic, self-satisfying, cruel son of a bitch to your face instead of just thinking it. Don't you remember when I couldn't say things like that? Just think them and feel them—but not *say* them?

SIDNEY   Which amounts to you paying that quack twenty dollars a session to teach you how to swear! Lots of luck!

IRIS   That's not the point!

SIDNEY   I'm sorry. Swear *out loud.*

IRIS (*Through her teeth*)   For someone who thinks that they are the great intellect of all times, the top-heaviest son of a bitch that ever lived—

SIDNEY (*Dryly*)   Another step toward mental health—

IRIS   For someone who thinks that they've got the most *open* mind that was ever opened—you are the most narrow-minded, provincial—

SIDNEY   —"insular and parochial"—

IRIS   —insular and parochial bastard alive! And I'll tell you this: I may be whacked up, sweetie, but I really would hate to see the inside of *your* stomach. *Oh-ho,* I really would! St. John of the Twelve Agonies, I'll tell you.

SIDNEY   I am not agonized.

IRIS   *Everyone* is agonized!

SIDNEY   How do you know this, Iris?

IRIS   *Everyone* knows it. *Der* (*She hesitates and mispronounces it*) *angst* is Everywhere. And I'll tell you this— if I had all your hostilities—

13

SIDNEY   Look, Iris, three years ago you practically tore up our marriage looking for a sex problem, because one fine day you decided we *had* to have one. We even *invented* one for six months because you *knew* we had to have one —because *everybody* did. Well, I promise you this time we are not going to embark on the search for my (*Correcting her*) angst!

IRIS (*Darkly. Sitting beside him on couch and teasing*)   I happen to know some things about you *in bed* that you don't know.

SIDNEY (*False and weary patience—but reaching out for her: he loves this girl*)   Then tell me about them so we can discuss them.

IRIS (*An air of the holy*)   Oh no! No siree. Get thyself to a professional. You're not going to catch *me* engaging in parlor analysis!

SIDNEY   There was no psychiatric mystery about it! It was almost purely technical. There were just things in bed I wished you *wouldn't* do—(*Huskily*)—and some I wished you would.
(*He holds her in his arms*)

IRIS (*In the sway of the moment*)   That just shows you: nothing about *sex* is *just* technical. (*Sitting up*)   And, I notice, *I'm* not the one around here with an ulcer. And I must say that for a *contented* man, who just *happens* to have an ulcer, you drink one hell of a lot!

SIDNEY   It's *my* ulcer! Moreover, I remember a time when, between the agonized and the contented, there was a *whole spectrum* of humanity.

IRIS (*Rather by rote*)   Basically you are an ambivalent personality. You can't admit to disorder of any sort because that symbolizes weakness to you, and you can't admit to health either because you associate that with superficiality...

SIDNEY   Oh shut the hell up! I can't stand it when you're on this jag!
> (*Reaching for her again: this precious foolishness is all a game he dearly loves*)

IRIS (*Shouting*)   Then why didn't you marry somebody you did like to talk to then!
> (*It hangs a second, is absorbed with minor melancholy by the husband, who, to rise above it, offers a parodied Elizabethan flourish*)

SIDNEY   Because—(*Lifting a drink like Cyrano*) "what did please the morning's academic ear did seem indeed— (*Bringing the hand down defeatedly*) to repel the evening's sensuous touch. Think this poor poet not cruel to say it; but—(*Concluding the flourish*) gentle Sid, be but a mortal thing."

IRIS (*Feminine cruelty*)   Awwww, is that what you told poor Evie when she proposed?

SIDNEY   She didn't propose. Cut it out.

IRIS   You once told me she did.

SIDNEY   Bedroom boasts. You don't pretend to believe mine and I won't pretend to believe yours. (*Holding her; in a quieter tone*) What you were supposed to say was, "In such regard and diluted esteem doth my master hold his own sweet Iris—"

IRIS (*Looking up*)   I don't know the piece. What is it?

SIDNEY (*Dully, staring off*)   Nothing.

IRIS   What?

SIDNEY   Plutarch or some damn body! What difference does it make *what* it's from?

IRIS   Well, whatever it's from, it said that you really do think I'm stupid!

SIDNEY (*Hardly to her at all*)   "My pardon on it, I will get me gone." (*A pause, then to her*) It said: I love you. It said I do not counsel reason or quarrel with my nature. It said, girl, that I love my wife. Curious thing.
(*Stops her lips with a kiss*)

IRIS   Meaning frivolous mind and all.

SIDNEY   You make a silly fishwife. Stop it.

IRIS   Can't I say *anything*?

SIDNEY   Not in this mood, it's driving me crazy!
(*He gets up agitatedly and goes to the window and looks out at the street*)

IRIS (*Resolute anger*)   And one thing is clear: You prefer picking at me to talking to me.

SIDNEY (*Shouting*)   I do not! And tell that Steiner to take his love-hate obsession and shove it!

IRIS   It is not something *you* can know about, Sid. I am talking about *unconscious* motivation.

SIDNEY   If it is all that "*un*" then you don't know about it either!

IRIS (*Puzzled; caught*) I meant "sub." A *sub*conscious motivation.

SIDNEY Look, let's talk about how we're going to get you to go to the audition.

IRIS (*Sore spot*) Sidney, why can't you understand about the blocks that people have?

SIDNEY (*Seated at his drawing board*) I do understand about them and I know that if they are nurtured and nourished enough they get bigger and bigger and bigger.

IRIS (*In kind, through her teeth*) All right, so I haven't worked out my life so good. Have you? Or are those glasses there a mere mirage I see before me?

SIDNEY Aw, what do you know about it?

IRIS (*Undulating away with triumph*) I know that there is no great wisdom in opening a folk-singing establishment where there are something like twenty of such establishments in a radius of four blocks square. I know that, darling-pie! And what the hell did you know about running a night club anyway?
(*She crosses into the bathroom to brush her teeth*)

SIDNEY (*Painfully: old refrain, lost cause*) It wasn't *supposed* to be a night club. (*A beat*) It *would* have done okay if Bruno had done a better job on the publicity.

IRIS (*Closes the bathroom door, and comes back*) He thought he should be paid.

SIDNEY I offered him a quarter of the place!

IRIS Who wants a quarter of a nonprofit night club?

SIDNEY *It wasn't a night club!*

IRIS And what are you going to do with all those glasses?

SIDNEY How do I know right now? There have to be other enterprises that need a hundred and fifty sturdy restaurant glasses, don't there?

IRIS When they audit the place they're going to think it's awfully funny that there're no glasses. What are you going to say happened to them?

SIDNEY How come I should know what happened to them? Why should I know every little detail. Maybe somebody broke in and took them or something.

IRIS Auditors like to know about the details, Sid. They specialize in the details.

SIDNEY And what are you worrying about that for? You oughta be glad I at least salvaged something out of it— that I had the get-up to go over there and get *something* out of there *before* they audit. Why can't you ever look at things that way? From the point of view of the things I do that have foresight. How come you gotta play wife-harpie all the time?
　　(IRIS *turns back the tracing paper on* SIDNEY's *board to reveal the masthead on which he had been working*)

IRIS (*Picking it up*) So now what? You're going to be an artist? This is *aw-ful.*
　　(*A fit of appropriate giggling*)

SIDNEY It's not supposed to be a drawing. It's the layout for the—

(*He halts, not having meant to get into this just this way*)

IRIS (*Already expecting almost anything*) For the *what*, Sidney?

SIDNEY (*He exhales heavily and sits*) Harvey Wyatt met some chick—

IRIS Yes, *and*—

SIDNEY —he decided to go live in Majorca. I mean forget the whole scene and just like that go live in Majorca . . .

IRIS (*Sitting, one hand over her lips*) Oh, my God, no . . . Sidney—*no*.

SIDNEY (*Shrugging*) So he *had* to unload the paper.

IRIS No. God, don't let it be true. Unload it on—*whom?* Oh, Sidney, you haven't . . . ?

SIDNEY I know it's hard for you, Iris. To understand what I'm all about—

IRIS (*Slumping where she is*) I don't believe this. I don't believe that you could come out of—of *that*—(*Gesturing to the glasses*) and get into *this*. Aside from anything else at the moment, what did you conceivably tell Harvey that you were going to pay him?

SIDNEY We made an arrangement. Don't worry about it.

IRIS What kind of arrangement, Sidney?

SIDNEY *An arrangement*. That's all. I know what I arranged. I tell you, don't worry about it, that's all.

IRIS   Where in the name of God are you going to get the money to pay for a newspaper?

SIDNEY   It's a *small* newspaper. A weekly.

IRIS   Sidney, you can't afford a *yearly leaflet!*

SIDNEY (*Quietly*)   Why isn't it ever enough for me to tell you that I know what I'm doing? The money was not the important part of the deal one way or the other. This is a real rich babe Harvey's hooked up with so he's not worried about the money just yet.

IRIS   And when he is—? Where are you going to get it? That's what little old Iris is standing here with her barefaced everyday-self wondering about.

SIDNEY   I'll raise it. That's all. I'll raise it. Period. Didn't I raise it for the Silver Dagger? Well, I'll raise it for this. In order to *do* things you have to *do* things. That's all.
(*During the above* WALLY O'HARA *and* ALTON SCALES *have approached; the former is a conventionally dressed man, in his early forties, with rust-colored thinning hair; he carries several cardboard placards. For a moment the two stand in animated conversation, as if planning their next move. Now* ALTON *beats on the door.* IRIS *throws up her hands in disgust and admits them*)

ALTON (*Kissing her broadly. Gesturing toward* WALLY) Hey, look who I ran into.

WALLY (*Shows a campaign poster to* SID *and* IRIS. *It reads:* VOTE O'HARA FOR REFORM) Hey, Sid.

SIDNEY (*Standing stock-still, resolutely*)   The answer is no.

ALTON (*Yelling at him*) Don't be a clown! At least hear what the man has to say!

WALLY Iris.
> (*He kisses her. She goes into the kitchen to make a salad*)

SIDNEY I know what he has to say and I don't want to hear it. I'm out of it. Period. My little artsy-craftsy newspaper is going to stay clear of politics. *Any* kind of politics. Politics are for people who have those kinds of interests, that's all. I don't happen to have them any more.

WALLY (*As if he expected that; making himself comfortable*) Yes, I know. You've made yourself clear in the past: "Politics are a blight on the natural spirit of man. Politics are a cancer of the soul. Politics are dirty, fetid, compromise-ridden exercises in futility." Et cetera, et cetera, et cetera. (*Wandering over to the glass racks and raising a glass*) A bunch of big drinkers here? (*Pouring a drink, then turning a knowing, skilled gaze on the editor*) Nonetheless, Sidney—I've finally faced up to something that you've got to face up to; there is work to be done and someone has got to do it. Now, I'm taking time out from a busy law practice which is just beginning to build. I'm sticking my neck out to run, and all I'm asking from you is a little legwork, and the endorsement of—what I take it is now—your paper.

SIDNEY Not even for you, Wally. My readers can do as they please. In my paper—no endorsements. And no editorials.

ALTON (*To* WALLY, *agitatedly*) You see! There it is, man! We are confronted with the great disease of the modern bourgeois intellectual: *ostrich*-ism. I've been watching it happen to this one; the great sad withdrawal from the affairs of men. (*With bitter facetiousness, pounding his breast—he pins up the poster on the bookshelves*) It sort of gets me, *here*.

SIDNEY   Alton, do you know that it is an absolute fact that the one infallible way that one can always, and I mean *always,* tell an ex-communist from ordinary human beings is by the sheer volume of his use of the word *bourgeois?*

ALTON   And do you know how one can always, infallibly, no matter what, tell a card-carrying phoney? By the minuteness of the pretext on which he will manage to change the subject, *if* the subject is even remotely important.

WALLY (*Laughing smoothly*)   Why do you boys hang out together?

SIDNEY (*Turning in kind on* ALTON)   Yes, I suppose I have lost the pretensions of the campus revolutionary, Alton. I do admit that I no longer have the energy, the purity or the comprehension to—"save the world." (*Takes down* WALLY's *poster. Looking at them with an internalized smile working the corners of his mouth*) As a matter of fact, to get *real big* about it, I no longer even believe that spring must necessarily come at all. Or, that if it does, that it will bring forth anything more poetic or insurgent than—(*With a flourish*) the winter's dormant ulcers.

WALLY (*Getting up, crossing to* SIDNEY. *There is a pervasive assurance about him*)   We're not talking about the world, we're talking about this community. It's like getting on the wagon, the way they tell you in the AA: Don't

think about all the drinks you've got to give up, just concentrate on the next one. That's the trick, Sid. Don't think
about the ailing world for the time being, just think about
your own little ailing neighborhood, that's the point.

SIDNEY (*Wandering away from him*)   That's very impressive. (*Hands the poster back to* WALLY) But the truth of
the matter is, dear friends, I am afraid that I have experienced the *death* of the exclamation point. It has died in
me. I no longer want to exhort anybody about anything.
It's the final end of boyhood: the death of the exclamation
point in my life. (*Grinning wryly at his friends*) Now, I
admit that this is something that doesn't happen to everyone. Take old Alton here: one *long* exclamation point!

ALTON (*Loftily*)   Capitulation has one smell, one shape,
one sound.

SIDNEY (*In kind*)   Look, I'm not a neophyte. You wanna
see my scrapbooks? Since I was eighteen I've belonged to
every committee To Save, To Abolish, Prohibit, Preserve,
Reserve and Conserve that ever was. And the result—
(*With an almost rollicking flippancy*) is that I can no
longer abide organization of any kind whatsoever; the
mere thought of a "movement" to do *anything* chills my
bones. I simply can no longer bear the spectacle of the
hatchery of power-driven insurgents trying at all costs to
gain control—(*The coup de grâce*) of the refreshment
committee!

    (*He crosses into the bathroom for a bottle of pills*)

WALLY (*Smiling easily*)   I told you: Think only of not taking the next drink.

SIDNEY (*Crossing back to the drawing board to take his pill with a drink*) You mean diddle around with the *little* things since we can't do anything about the *big* ones? Like the fact that I was born of a father who was maimed in one war, did some fighting of my own in another and have survived into the clear and present danger of a third? Forget about all that jazz, huh, and worry about—reforms in the traffic court or something?

WALLY (*Putting his drink down, with vigor*) Christ, man, this is the second largest narcotics drop in the city, the outpost of every racket known to man! The syndicate thinks it owns this neighborhood, and there sits the regular machine—

SIDNEY You kid yourself if you want to, Wally. *Do things* if it makes you happy. Just don't bug me about it. Iris, beer!

IRIS (*Coming out from the kitchen*) All I've got to say, Sidney, is just mean what you say, that's all, just *mean* what you say.

WALLY (*Strictly in jest*) All of which goes to prove that a woman's place is in the oven.

ALTON (*Mugging*) *With* the door closed.

WALLY I'm wondering, Sidney. In the clear and present danger—
      (*The phone is ringing*)

IRIS Jesus, that'll be Mavis. I don't feel like Mavis tonight. Sid, you get it.

SIDNEY   I never feel like Mavis. You get it. (*Iris goes to answer*) That Mavis, boy—I *still* swear she is something Sinclair Lewis made up which has escaped the book! (*Looking at* ALTON *soberly*) Speaking of Iris' sisters, I gather you've been seeing a lot of Gloria when she's in town.

> (IRIS, *at the phone, throws a swift pregnant glance at her husband*)

ALTON   (*Mugging heavily and smacking his lips*) Yeaaahhhh.

SIDNEY   Yeah, well, take it from me and beware of the daughters of the House of Atreus.

> (IRIS *looks daggers*)

ALTON   (*Glibly, unaware of the by-play*) I'll take my chances. (*To* WALLY) You should *see* this one, man!

> (*Waving his fingers for the heat*)

WALLY   (*Smiling*)   I'd like to. (*Back to the attack*) Sidney, if you can't function—

ALTON   Only there's no point in your meeting her *now*, man. Like *I* have come into her vision and I am filling it out *entirely!*

WALLY   So where is this perfection? Why doesn't she drop by and help restore Sidney's vision?

IRIS (*Cutting in, one hand cupping the receiver*)   She's in Los Angeles. Travels a lot. She's a high-fashion model. (ALTON *passes a photo of* GLORIA *to* SID *and* WALLY) I *am* listening to you, love. I don't care, Mav, that's all. Goodbye! (*As she hangs up the phone and wanders back to a position near her husband*) Poor old Mavis. But you've got to admit that she doesn't give up. She's been trying to civilize me for years. Now she's got some dress for me.

SIDNEY   Dear old Mav, Mother of the Philistines. My brother is the Prince, but your sister is the Mother of them all!

(*He suddenly pulls the pins out of his wife's hair, causing it to fall down all over her. She is infuriated by this habit of his*)

IRIS   Oh, damn it, Sid! Don't start that, I'm telling you! I mean it!

ALTON (*To* WALLY)   If he had his way he'd have her running barefoot in a gingham dress with all that hair flying around. (*To* SIDNEY) What are you, some kind of arrested rustic?

WALLY   I've often wondered how such a nice middle-classed Jewish boy got so hung up on such a tired old Anglo-Saxon myth.

SIDNEY (*Western drawl*)   I reckon my particular Jewish psyche was less discriminating than most.

WALLY (*Pressing forward*)   Sidney, if you can't function in one little community, then how—

SIDNEY (*Escaping again*)   Hey, honey, you know what I feel like? I am suddenly suffering from an all-consuming desire to take my books, my cameras, my records, and— my wife—and go—

IRIS, ALTON *and* WALLY (*Together, in unison*)   —up to the woods!

(*She, without appreciation, starts working at her hair, trying to get it back up*)

SIDNEY (*Painfully*) Yes. And stay . . . (*Pulling her head back hard and looking into her eyes*) Forever.
(*She sighs*)

ALTON (*To* WALLY) Man, you see what we are up against here? This clown is not only committed to the symbolic mountain tops. He goes in for the *whole real live physical thing*.

SIDNEY (*Changing the subject; to* ALTON) By the way, I made an appointment with Mickey Dafoe for you. He expects you in his office at noon. Wear a tie and your best Establishment Ass-kissing Manner or something so you won't make him nervous.

ALTON What do you mean you made an appointment for me? For what? What do I want to see Mickey Dafoe for?

SIDNEY Gotta be you. Nobody else to go.

ALTON Well, there's not me, I have nothing to say to people like Mickey Dafoe.

SIDNEY You're right, you're wrong for it. Absolutely the wrong man to send. The Trade and Commerce Association is only responsible for like half of the advertising in the paper. We need somebody—(*Moving "aimlessly" toward* WALLY *so that at the last word they are face to face.* WALLY *is already shaking his head "no"*) smoo-ooooth.

WALLY Don't look at me.

SIDNEY   Why not, you fat cat you—?

WALLY   What makes you think you can always ask, ask, ask for things, Sid—and never give?

SIDNEY   (*Throwing up his hands*)   Because before I am through my little artsy-craftsy newspaper is going—

IRIS   Oh, Sidney, newspaper, newspaper, newspaper! How long do you think that you're going to *have* a newspaper! (*She disappears into the bedroom, putting her hair up*)

ALTON   What's the matter with her lately?

SIDNEY   (*A shrug*)   Who knows? Maybe she's changing life.

WALLY   Come on, it's the Greek in her. You should know that. The triumph of the innate tragedy in her soul.

SIDNEY   (*This entire exchange is for* IRIS *to hear*)   She's only half Greek, so she should be only half tragic. Hey, Iris, when you come back out, turn up just one side of your face.

IRIS   Boy, are you fellows fun-nee! (*A wild cackle of sardonic laughter*)

WALLY   Hey, what is the other half?

SIDNEY   Irish 'n' Cherokee. I'm married to the only Greco-Gaelic-Indian hillbilly in captivity. If one can really think of Iris as being in captivity . . . Do your dance, honey. (*She snakes out promptly, hissing, in the dance steps of the Greek Miserlou—which turns into a jig and then into the usual stereotyped notion of some Indian war dance, concluding with a Marilyn Monroe freeze. Then she backs out)* I taught her everything she knows! You should hear my mother on Iris. *(The inevitable)* "Not that I have anything against the goyim, Sidney, she's a nice girl, but the rice is too greasy. And *lamb* fat? For the *stomach?* With hominy grits? *Like a lump it sits.*"

WALLY *(Nodding toward where* IRIS *is)* Any shows coming up?

SIDNEY *(Softly, hand up to discourage the subject)* Don't bring it up.

ALTON *(Who has been flipping the pages of a book on the coffee table in front of him)* One of your troubles is, Sid, that you admire the wrong parts of Thoreau.

SIDNEY *(Who is deep in the chair; his back to* ALTON, *hand behind his head)* How do you know what parts of Thoreau I do or don't admire?

ALTON You mark passages—*(He promptly starts to read aloud, while roaming the room, meaning in the beginning to inflict the facetious taunt on it, trilling his r's, but ultimately finding some difficulty in it, perhaps as the words have appeal even to him. As he reads we are aware of certain familiar colorings and inflections in his speech though we cannot presently place them)* ". . . In the coldest and bleakest places, the warmest charities still maintain a foothold. A cold and searching wind drives away all contagion, and nothing can withstand it but what has virtue in it. Whatever we meet in cold and bleak places, as the tops of mountains—" See! Always looking for them *mountain tops!* (IRIS *crosses into the kitchen, re-*

turns and sits shelling a bowl of peas) "We respect for a sort of sturdy innocence. . . . It is invigorating to breathe the cleansèd air . . . and we fain would stay out long and late, that the gales may sigh through us, too, as through the lifeless trees, and fit us for the winter:—as if we hoped so to borrow some pure and steadfast virtue which will stead us in all seasons."

> *(SIDNEY takes the book from him thoughtfully and a little defiantly, snaps it shut and returns it to its place on the shelf, then sits looking off)*

WALLY   All right—how's about the rest of Thoreau, Sidney boy? How's about the Thoreau of sublime social consciousness, the Thoreau who was standing in jail one day when that holy of holies, Mr. Ralph Waldo Emerson, comes strolling by and asks, "Well, Henry, what are you doing in there?" And Thoreau, who was "in there" for protesting the evils of his day, looked out at him and said—"The question is, Ralph, what are you doing (*New England old-timer inflection*) out thay-ah?"

> *(IRIS knowing SIDNEY only too well and sensing the drift, starts humming "The Battle Hymn of the Republic")*

SIDNEY   Cut it out.

ALTON   *(Coolly plunging in for the kill)*   Why, Sid? She's right . . . Wally, stop that foolishness! Cool it, man. You're "venerating"! You're "celebrating the human spirit"! Your "*conscience* is showing"! Don't you know, Wally, "Readers—(*Indicating* IRIS) don't want it." The great untutored public—(*Indicating the window*) doesn't want it. And what's more, the exhausted insurgent—(*Indicating*

SIDNEY) cannot afford it. 'S no use, Wally: the man's in mourning for his boyhood. Let's go before he sells you one hundred and fifty restaurant glasses.

(*He gets up*)

SIDNEY (*Stung*) Well, hooray the hell for you! . . . John the Baptist! (*He throws himself onto his knees and with outstretched arms offers a slow and very precise salaam*) God bless your Saviour-type soul!

(*Hands fluttering holy-roller style, he begins a wailing chant, which peters out as* ALTON *stands over him, relentless*)

ALTON Look out, man, you're getting overinvolved. Too emotional; you might *shed a tear*. After all, what is it? Only one kid. One lousy junkie, all of seventeen. (*Brutally offhand*) What'd he do, sweep for you at the Silver Dagger, whatever his name is?

SIDNEY (*Softly*) Sal Peretti . . .

ALTON Oh yeah—Sal Peretti.

SIDNEY I did what I could—

IRIS (*Furious, pleading to hold back the inevitable*) Sidney, you gave him a job—you can't be responsible for *every strange kid that walks in off the street!*

SIDNEY I tried to help.

(IRIS *exits into the kitchen*)

ALTON Let's go, Wally, we're wasting time.

(*Pulling* WALLY *after him*)

WALLY (*At the door*) I'm counting on you, Sid.

SIDNEY Don't.

> (*They exit.* SIDNEY *sits at his drawing board for a long moment. Then he crosses to the glasses. He puts one foot up on the cases and cups his chin in his hand, as his eye falls on the discarded poster*)

SIDNEY (*Musing*) Iris ... do you think my brother Manny would support a reform candidate if I made him a present of one hundred and fifty sturdy restaurant glasses?

IRIS (*Rushes out of the kitchen clutching a dripping head of lettuce*) Sidney, I swear to heaven—I'll poison you!

Blackout

John Alderman, Alice Ghostley, Gabriel Dell, Rita Moreno, and Ben Aliza
as DAVID RAGIN, MAVIS BRYSON, SIDNEY BRUSTEIN, IRIS BRUSTEIN
and ALTON SCALES

Scene Two

Time: Dusk. The following week. In the darkness before the lights come up, once again the quarrelsome voices are heard.

MAX (*Round, juicy, gravel-voiced*) Sca-rrew Michelangelo! You and Michelangelo all the time! Christ! Not again . . .

ALTON Yes, again. The *larger* statement has to say it *all*— (*The lights come up.* ALTON *and* MAX *are in the apartment. The latter's free-form paintings, laid out for inspection about the place, have inspired the present violent discussion.* MAX *is by all odds an original: middle-aged, gravel-voiced, squat, his salt-and-pepper short hair brushed dead forward; he wears sandals, stained jeans, a black turtleneck and a pained expression*)

MAX Your main trouble is that you are a literalist. You were born a literalist and you will die a literalist.

ALTON And all I am saying is that decay is *not* the deepest damn thing going, you know? It's sick—so, like, it's supposed to be pro*found?* Too easy, baby. Death is too damn easy. Chaos is easier. And when you pretend that *that* is the scale of existence—

MAX (*Gesture of the streets*) Go the hell away, Alton. You don't know a damn thing except *poster* art.

33

ALTON What old poster art! Is Leonardo poster art?

MAX (*Slamming down something with outrage*) I knew it, here we go again: back to the frigging Renaissance! (SIDNEY *enters carrying a large banner*)

SIDNEY I got it.

ALTON Great. Let's put it up, I've already got the nails in. (SIDNEY *flings one end to* ALTON *and they hold it, for a moment unfurled. It reads:*

CLEAN UP COMMUNITY POLITICS

Wipe Out Bossism

VOTE REFORM

(*They stride to the window—where, presently, it hangs, face out to the street*)

SIDNEY All right, let's go to work. (*He sits at his board,* ALTON *at his side.* MAX *sits benignly apart: the "man of the hour," awaiting the call*) Now, with a new masthead, the front page will stay pretty much as it is. Page two, some jumps and lesser items . . . page three, interviews, you know. Page four, letters to the editor and some weekly artwork.

ALTON (*Winks—the victor*) And the editorials.

SIDNEY (*Toss-off—who ever denied it? Then laughs*) And the editorials. Five and six: theatre, dance and movie reviews. By the way, I want to get rid of Dan Wallace and get Paul Russo. He's good.

ALTON If you like obscurity, he's the best.

SIDNEY Sure, Russo gets a little fuzzy, but you've got to admit the man knows films. (*As if this were somehow relevant*) He's a very gentle man. Do you know he wanders around with little bits and pieces of paper in his pocket on which he writes down every single thing that moves him, good or bad, in a day?

ALTON And at the end of the week he puts them in a hat and stirs them—and that's his movie review for the week!

SIDNEY Oh, Alton, knock off! Where's the masthead, Max?
(MAX *rises and crosses ceremoniously with his portfolio; he opens it and places the masthead before them. Then, with a flourish, he flips off the tracing paper to unveil it, and stands back*)

MAX (*Modestly*) Here. It's a rough idea, you know.
(SIDNEY *and* ALTON *squint at it hard, look at each other, puzzled; the two turn it sidewise and upside down.* MAX *restores it rightside up. The two squint again. Finally,* ALTON *points to the bottom of the page*)

SIDNEY Three-point type for the nameplate of a newspaper? At the bottom of the page? Who's going to see it?

MAX (*Columbus Incarnate, Galileo, Copernicus, the Wright Brothers and Frank Lloyd, in one*) That's the whole point. You put it far right and low on the big field—and the eye *has* to follow. (*Professor to slow pupil, guides their eyes down and around the page with a finger. The other two men are silent;* MAX *is offended and starts to gather his things*)

SIDNEY Max, I like it—it just occurred to me—I like it!

35

MAX (*Petulant, undeterred*)   Look, I thought it was something different, something fresh.
(*He starts out*)

SIDNEY   But, Max—

MAX   It's always that way. You revolutionaries are all the same. You start out full of fire and end up full of . . . shit!
(*He exits.* SIDNEY *rises*)

ALTON   Oh, Sidney! I'm telling you, it looks like a bunch of art majors from Music and Art designed that page.

SIDNEY   Alton, will you please! (*Follows* MAX *out—takes the masthead from* MAX, *studies it*) Max, you've done it again!

MAX (*One more moment of immovable glory; then relents*) As a matter of fact, Sid, let's change it every week. (SIDNEY *and* MAX *re-enter and cross to the board*) You know, a different type—Old English, Gothic, Bodoni. However we feel the day we're making it up.

SIDNEY   Max—you're so creative!

MAX   And in a different place! Locate it on a different place on the sheet every week!

ALTON (*Suddenly shouting*)   It's a newspaper! It's a goddamned newspaper—not an avant-garde toy!

MAX   He doesn't change, does he? You know, once you've had that Marxist monkey on your back you're hooked for life. To Alton—a newspaper's not an aesthetic adventure, it's— (*He tightens his face and balls his fist in a mock-serious gesture*) a weapon! (*Carried away by his idea, he*

leaps on the couch with an imaginary banner and sings)
" 'Tis the final conflict
Let each stand in his place—
The international—"

ALTON Aw, go to hell.

MAX *(Sings)* "Unites the human race!"
    (IRIS enters and halts at the sight. She is in her uniform, carrying paella in a brown paper bag)

IRIS *(Violent facetiousness)* Well, *company.* And who have I invited to supper tonight?
    (She has their attention at last)

ALTON Paella?
    (She nods "yes," with eyes closed, knowing that he will stay now. He puts his hand in the air to deliberately affect the class-room mannerism of a small child)

IRIS Max?

MAX *(Still on the couch)* Paella. Like crazy. *(Rubbing his head, stomach and consulting his watch, genuinely conflicted)* But the problem is . . . there's this chick I was *supposed* to have met in the Black Knight, Jesus, an hour ago . . .

SIDNEY There it is: the primeval decision, food or sex.
    (MAX closes his eyes to imagine a little of each presumably, caught in the pose of the true primitive)

ALTON *(Going and leaning under MAX more or less to study the decision)* And let us watch *primitive* man decide—
    (MAX opens his eyes, steps down from the couch and

37

begins to gather up his things in order to make the prior date. IRIS *exits into the bedroom*)

ALTON   The *loins* triumph! See, Max, you're *not* a true primitive or you would have put *food* first! You only *paint* like a savage. (*Pursuing* MAX *to the door*) And— where the hell did you get that outfit, man? You look just like a put-up job for *Life*-Magazine-Visits-the-Left-Bank-and-all. Where's your goatee?

MAX (*Staring him down—a squelch*)   That's the difference between me and you, Alton: I have finally become a truly free man. I have even stopped worrying about *not* trying to look like a nonconformist *not* nonconforming. Dig?
(*He exits, giving* ALTON *one last baby chuck on the chin.* IRIS *re-enters from bedroom in jeans and a sweater, with mail*)

IRIS   Hey, I got a letter from Gloria.

ALTON   How is life in the pancake world, Iris, my light?

IRIS (*Reading her mail*)   Be still. I gotta read my mail. (ALTON *takes the banjo down, crosses to the rocker, begins to pick the banjo . . .* IRIS *looks up from the letter slowly, with astonishment and many confusions in her face*) Why, Alton Scales . . . Gloria says that you asked her to marry you.

ALTON (*Affecting the bashful teenager*)   Yup.

SIDNEY (*Looks up at him and then at his wife, and then back to his friend*)   Are you for real?

ALTON (Ibid.)   Yup.

SIDNEY   You're that gone on her?

38

ALTON (*Sudden lover's hoarse sincerity*) In fact, I figure that if that babe doesn't hurry up and get herself back here—like I could flip.

SIDNEY I'll be damned. (*To his wife*) You never know.

IRIS (*In astonishment*) You never know.

SIDNEY What did she say: "yes" or "no"?

ALTON She didn't. She said she'd think about it while she was away—(*Strumming out an accompaniment on the banjo for emphasis*)—and like I have been *living* with tension for two weeks! (*Abruptly, his strum breaks into "The Midnight Special!" and he sings. After a few lines he stops. As the silence dawns on him—tensely*) What's the matter? (*The other two avoid replying in an awkward moment of misunderstood discomfort.* SIDNEY *re-concentrates on his board;* IRIS *just sits, not knowing what to say.* ALTON, *tightly, with mounting anger, speaks directly to* SIDNEY, *crossing to him and standing fully in front of him; angrily*) I said what's the matter, goddamnit! Come on, let's have it out, my little gray friends! This is like the moment of truth, old babies! Yeah, come on! Let's get to the nitty gritty, as it were! Let's blast all the crap away—

IRIS Oh, Alton!

SIDNEY (*Simply*) Why don't you take that damn tree off your shoulder, Alton? Frankly, it's embarrassing.
    (*They glare at one another;* ALTON *softens to a different kind of embarrassment*)

ALTON Well, don't expect me to apologize . . . I have a right to think anything I want. In *this* world. Even of *you*—Sid.

SIDNEY   There are some misunderstandings that cost more than others, Alton.

IRIS   Besides, the point is—well—for crying out loud—who'd expect that you two? Well, you know what I mean: You're so Paul P. Proletarian and all, and she's the Living Spirit of Madison Avenue.

ALTON   Well, hell, opposites attract and all, to coin a phrase. Besides, like—(*Slowly, real slow*) I dig her!

SIDNEY (*With great sobriety*)   That much?

ALTON (*A lover*)   *That* much!

SIDNEY (*Russian accent*)   Another bolshevik bites the dust.

IRIS (*Her eyes on him intently*)   And that's all that we have to say about it, isn't it, Sidney?

SIDNEY (*Considering swiftly and accepting this judgment*)   That's all.

IRIS   Where's my *Variety*?

SIDNEY (*Back with his board*)   Under the apples.

IRIS (*A long afterthought*)   And I don't like that expression, come to think of it.

SIDNEY   What expression?

IRIS (*Shaking her finger, not serious*)   About biting the dust. I know where that came from. And on behalf of my Cherokee grandfather, I protest.

ALTON   I got your point, so knock it off.

IRIS (*Turning on him*)   You knock it off, sometimes, Alton! It's a bore. You and the causes all the time. It's phoney as hell!

ALTON (*Sharply, back at her*) I was born with *this* cause.

IRIS That's what I mean! Fun with illusion and reality: white boy playing black boy all the time.

ALTON I *am* a black boy. I didn't make up the game, and as long as a lot of people think there is something wrong with the fact that I *am* a Negro—I am going to make a point out of being one. Follow!

IRIS (*Pragmatic bohemia*) But that's what makes it so phoney. The country is full of people who dropped it when they could—what makes you so ever-loving different?

ALTON It's something you either understand or don't understand.
    (*He shrugs*)

IRIS Well, I guess everybody has to do *something* with their guilts.

ALTON (*Flaring*) Guilt's got nothing to do with it . . .

SIDNEY Come on, this is a stupid conversation. Be a Martian if you wanna.

IRIS (*Settling down with her* Variety. *Whistling it out*) Heroes, heroes, everywhere—and not a battle won! (ALTON *rises, abruptly—quickly crosses to the door*) Alton?

ALTON (*Turning at the door—gruff, indirect apology*) I'm going out for some wine for my contribution to the feed. Want something? Cigarettes?

SIDNEY (*Grinning*) Nope.

ALTON   How about you, Laughing Tomahawk?
(*He exits*)

IRIS   Flowers. For the table. (*Follows him out the door—
calls after him*) If you're going to be a brother-in-law you
should try to get in with me. I know *plenty* about being a
sister-in-law. Bring me flowers every day . . . (*At the top of
her lungs*) Lumumba. (*She ducks as the paperback he has
been reading comes crashing against the door frame. She
comes back in, closing the door. At once to her husband,
sharply, wife-ishly*) You just keep your mouth shut about
Gloria, you hear!

SIDNEY   Did I say anything?

IRIS   No, but you sat there looking like death. Let them
work it out, see! Let them work it out. Keep your mouth
off it, I'm telling you.

SIDNEY   (*Almost screaming, as the point has been made*)
Did I say anything, did I say anything, *shrew?*

IRIS   (*Turning back to her paper*)   No, but I know you—
the world's biggest busybody. (SIDNEY *rises, crosses, hands
her the new masthead and, like the cat that swallowed the
canary, unveils it with same proud flourish as* MAX. IRIS
sits blankly, squints, looks at SIDNEY, *turns it sidewise and
upside down; finally he rights it and guides her eye in
almost exact repetition of the prior sequence*) You keeping it a secret? Looks arty.

SIDNEY   (*Furious*)   All right—so it looks arty. What does
that mean, do you know?

IRIS   Do I know what?

SIDNEY Do you know what "arty" means? Or is it just some little capsule phrase thrown out to try to diminish me, since you have nothing genuinely analytical or even observant to say?
(*He is staring at her hard, angrily*)

IRIS I wasn't trying to be analytical. I was saying what I thought, which is that it looks arty.

SIDNEY You mean that it looks different from other publications.

IRIS No, I mean it looks different from other publications in a self-conscious sort of way. *Arty*.

SIDNEY Iris, where did you get the idea you know enough about these things to pass judgment on them?

IRIS From the same place you got the idea that you were an editor.

SIDNEY Which happens at least to be more reasonable than the idea that you are anybody's actress.

IRIS (*Putting down her paper, slowly, hurtfully*) Why don't you just hit me with your fists sometimes, Sid.
(*Exits into the bathroom. Sobs are heard*)

SIDNEY I didn't mean that, baby. Come on. Do *South Pacific*. I'll hold the book for you.

IRIS No.
(*More sobs*)

SIDNEY Iris, honey, come on.
(*He opens the door—she pulls it shut. After a moment he tries again and she, clutching the inner knob, is tugged half into the room*)

43

IRIS (*Flaring irrationally, crossing out and down*) Why should I go through all of that to read for something that I know I won't get in the first place. They don't want actresses, they just want easy lays, that's all. (*Snarling*) That Harry Maxton, *please!* He's the biggest lech of them all. You want to know something, you really want to hear something I hope will burn your little ears off? That's why I didn't get the part before. I said "no"!
> (SIDNEY *has halted and is standing, half turned from her, letting it pour out of her as he has many, many times before*)

SIDNEY (*Turning quietly, almost gently*) Iris, everybody knows that Harry Maxton is one of the most famous fags in America.

IRIS All right, then. So everything goes with him! He just puts on the fag bit to cover up what he really is—

SIDNEY (*With proper incredulity*) You mean a lech?

IRIS (*With a wild, cornered gesture*) Sure, that's how twisted up they are in show business, you just don't know!

SIDNEY (*Helplessly*) Even in show business—that twisted they're not. And making up sordid excuses to yourself is not the solution to your problem, so come off it!

IRIS Leave me alone, Sidney. I don't want the part.
> (*She has curled into a tight sulking ball*)

SIDNEY (*Continuing on, getting the book and then crossing back to her and kneeling in front of her*) Oh, Iris, Iris, Iris . . . (*He puts his head wearily on her knee*) I want to help . . . so much . . . I'm on your side.

IRIS   I just don't have it. They say if you really have it—
you stick with it no matter what—and that—that you'll
do anything—

SIDNEY   That is one of the great romantic and cruel ideas
of our civilization. A lot of people "have it" and they
just get trampled to death by the mob trying to get up the
same mountain.

IRIS   Oh—please, Sidney, don't start blaming everything
on society. Sooner or later a person learns to hold *himself*
accountable—that's what maturity is. If I haven't learned
anything else in analysis I've sure learned that.

SIDNEY   Thank you, Dr. Steiner! Look, Iris, the world's
finest swimmer cannot swim the Atlantic Ocean—even if
analysis *does* prove it was his mother's fault!

IRIS   That's not an analogy. *Nobody* can swim the Atlantic
Ocean—but some people *do* make it in the theatre. (*She
smiles at him and puts her hand on his head and he settles
at her feet*) You make the lousiest analogies. Just like you
can't add. I couldn't believe that at first.

SIDNEY   What?

IRIS   About your arithmetic. When I first met you I thought
you were putting me on. You know, anybody all *that*
brilliant who couldn't *add*. God, at home almost *nobody*
could read—but *everybody* could add. (*Looking at him
and playing with his hair a little*) What's seven and
seven—?

SIDNEY   Fourteen, naturally.

IRIS (*Quickly*)   And fourteen and fourteen?

SIDNEY (*Hesitates. She giggles and he nestles playfully against her legs*) Twenty-eight.

IRIS And twenty-eight and twenty-eight?

SIDNEY (*Abruptly lost*) Oh, c'mon. That's calculus . . .
(*Both laugh; he comes into her arms*)

IRIS You don't know what it's like though—(*She is looking off, moving her fingers through his hair*) God, to walk through those agency doors . . . There's always some gal sitting on the other side, at a desk, you know, with a stack of pictures practically up to the ceiling in front of her. And they're always sort of bored, you know. Even the polite ones, the nice ones, I mean, they can't help it. They've seen five million and two like you and by the time you come through that door they are *bored*. And when you get past them, into the waiting room, there they are—the five million and two sitting there, waiting to be seen, and they look scared and mean and as competitive as you do. And so you all sit there, and you don't know anything: how you look, how you feel, anything. And least of all do you know how they *want* you to read. And when you get inside, you know less. There are just those faces, Christ, half the time you almost wish that someone *would* make a pass or something; you could deal with that, you know—that's from *life*. You can deal with that and take your chances, but that almost never happens, at least not to me. All I ever see are those blank director-producer-writer faces just staring at you like a piece of unfinished wood, waiting for you to show them something that will excite them, get them to arguing about you . . . And you just stand there knowing that you *can't*, no matter what, *do* it the way you *did* at home in front of the mirror, the brilliant imaginative way you did it the night before. No matter what. All you can think is: What the hell am I doing standing here in front of these strangers like some kind of damned fool, reading these silly words and jumping around for that fairy like some kind of nut . . . ? (*Looking up at him*) Sidney, I wish I had it in me to—to be *tougher*. (*Gently*) Like—like Gloria, I guess.

SIDNEY   Gloria wasn't tough *enough*, but let's not get into that.

IRIS   No, let's not! Anyhow, this is all a waste of time. You know and I know that I will never show up for that audition. I just don't want to see those doors again—Jesus, do I ever feel *twenty-nine!*

SIDNEY   Take down your hair for me, Iris . . .

IRIS   (*Hoarsely, but not angrily*)   Christ, you're still so hooked on my hair . . . (*Laughter through tears*) It's spooky to be loved for your hair, don't you know that?

SIDNEY   Take down your hair . . . (*He reaches up behind and pulls the pins and it falls and there really is a great deal of it which almost covers her. Then he gets up and crosses to the phonograph, puts on a record and turns and waits; in a second or two a stinging mountain banjo hoedown cuts into the silence. It swells and races: louder, swifter, filling room and theatre, this untamed music of the Bluegrass; in all the world there is none more vibrant*) Dance for me, Iris Parodus . . . Come down out of the hills and dance for me, Mountain Girl.

47

IRIS (*Lifting up her eyes to him from behind the hair*)   I just don't feel Appalachian tonight, Sid. It just won't work tonight—(*They look at one another a long moment. The music continues. During the above,* MAVIS BRYSON, IRIS' *older sister, has crossed to the door. She is a heavier, red-headed version of* IRIS, *more uptown and fashionable. She knocks and* IRIS *gets up and opens the door—then, as swiftly, shuts and bars it with her outstretched body. Meaning the dress box which her sister is carrying:*) I don't want it, I don't need it and I won't take it.

MAVIS   Just try it on. That's all I ask. (IRIS *reluctantly opens the door to admit her*) Hello, Sid, darling.

SIDNEY   Hello, Mav.

MAVIS (*Blithely opens the box*)   Could you conceivably have the hootenanny at another time?
(*She turns off the phonograph*)

IRIS   We don't go to cocktail parties, Mavis. At least the kind where you dress like *that*. I want to tell you from the top, Mavis. This is not a good time. I am in no mood for the big sister–little sister hassle today—that's all—
(MAVIS *crosses and maternally stops* IRIS' *mouth in mid-speech with one hand*)

MAVIS   Just slip it on; I had it taken up for you. You'll look stunning in it. (*Confidentially, as she zips and buttons*) What's that awful sign? Iris, it looks so vulgar to have writing in your window. (IRIS *points to* SID *as the culprit*) What have you heard from Gloria?

IRIS   Not a word.

48

MAVIS Here, let me smooth it down on you. Now, really, I can't tell a thing with those sticking out. (IRIS *pulls up her jeans as far as possible under the dress*) It's stunning! (*As, in fact, it is, because, whatever else,* MAVIS' *taste is simple and elegant and the dress* will *be handsome on* IRIS) Now, all you'll need for Easter is a new pair of sneakers.

SIDNEY (*Appreciatively*) You're coming along, Mavis, you're coming along. How about a drink?
(*He goes to the bar*)

MAVIS You know, you're drinking a lot lately, Sidney. (*To* IRIS) I thought you always said that the Jews didn't drink.

SIDNEY (*Crossing from the bar*) Mavis, I'm assimilated!

MAVIS Where was Gloria when you heard from her?

IRIS Miami Beach. (*Then, angry with herself*) And you're turning into a pure sneak—when it comes to digging.

MAVIS And you weren't going to tell me. (*To* SIDNEY) Why can't she tell me? Miami Beach, my God! (*A beat*) Is she—?

IRIS Of course she is, what do you think!

MAVIS (*Fingers to eyes*) The poor baby. All I can think of is that I am so glad Papa didn't live to—

IRIS Look, Mavis, don't start. I just don't want the Gloria problem tonight. No matter what else—she is living *her* life and we are living *ours.* (*A beat*) So to speak.
(*She exits into the bedroom*)

49

MAVIS Is she coming any time soon?

IRIS She didn't say.
   (*She enters again*)

MAVIS When?

IRIS Why can't you leave it alone, Mav? She won't see you
   when she does come. I guess she just can't take all those
   lectures any more.

MAVIS And you don't lecture her—do you?

IRIS (*Pouring a drink*) Mavis, if you weren't the world's
   greatest living anti-Semite you really should have married
   Sidney so that the two of you could have minded the
   world's business together. Jees!

MAVIS That's not funny and I am not, for the four thou-
   sandth time, an anti-Semite. (*Swiftly*) You don't think
   that about me, do you, Sid? Why?

IRIS Now, come on: you nearly had a heart attack when
   we got married. In fact, that's when you went into
   analysis. Now either you were madly in love with me or
   you hate the Jews—*pick!*

MAVIS (*Glaring at her*) Sometimes, Iris . . . (*A beat*) Did
   she say if she needs anything?

IRIS Now, what could *she* need? She's the successful one.
   As a matter of fact—(*Winks*) I plan to put the old touch
   on her when she comes back.

MAVIS Iris, you've gotten to be just plain dirty-minded.

IRIS Look, I happen to have a sister who is a fancy call girl,
   a big-time, high-fashion whore. And I say so what? She's

racking up thousands of tax-free dollars a year and it's her life so—who's to say?

(*Having done with responsibility, she shrugs with confidence*)

MAVIS (*Plaintively*) It's your baby sister—how can you talk like that?

IRIS Look, Mav, you're all hung up in the puritan ethic and all. That's not my problem.

MAVIS (*Gazing at her*) Is anything?

IRIS Frankly, it's an anti-sex society—

SIDNEY (*Exploding: enough is enough*) Oh, shut up! I can't stand it when you start prattling every lame-brained libertarian slogan that comes along without knowing what the hell you're talking about.

IRIS (*With great indignation*) I am entitled to my opinion, Sid-nee!

SIDNEY (*Riding over her*) You are *not*! Not so long as your opinion is based on stylish ignorance!

IRIS Oh shut up, Sidney. On this subject you are the last of the Victorians.

SIDNEY Not at all. You give old Victoria too much credit. If there was anything Victorians believed in it was that there *was* a place for the whore in society. The Victorians, sweet, were not against "sin," they were opposed to its *visibility*.

MAVIS The *things* you *think* you have to talk about!

IRIS All I know is this is an anti-sex soci—

SIDNEY   Look, Iris love— (*He grabs his head with frustration, wanting to make himself understood*) how can I put it to you, in front of Mavis, so that you get it? (MAVIS *rolls her eyes offendedly*) Victoria is dead so—like—it's just not that hard to *have* it, if you know what I mean, with your own girl friend. Dig? The guys running to the call girls are not pushing the sex revolution you think you are cheer-leading—they are indulging in a medieval notion of its disrespectability! Aside from which, there ought to be some human relationships on which commerce cannot put its grisly paws, doncha think?

IRIS   Who cares? My whole point is that I just don't care.

MAVIS   Sidney, Gloria is a very sick girl. She's not bad. She's very, very sick.

IRIS   Well, she's in analysis, for crying out loud! (*Both turn and look at her, MAVIS blankly, SIDNEY triumphant*) Well, she *says* he's helping her . . .

SIDNEY (*Eyeing MAVIS; to IRIS—cat and mouse*)   Oh, Iris, why don't you tell her the new development?

MAVIS (*To SIDNEY*)   What?

IRIS (*To SIDNEY*)   Fat mouth.

MAVIS (*Wheeling to her sister*)   What—?

IRIS (*To MAVIS, after another beat*)   There's somebody we know who wants to marry her.

MAVIS (*Closing her eyes and leaning back as if some particular prayer has been answered at exactly this moment*) Praise his name! (*Opening her eyes*) Who? (*Anxiously—*

to SIDNEY) One of your friends? (*He nods "yes." To* IRIS)
What does he do?

SIDNEY (*Almost laughing*) Well, as a matter of fact, he
works in a bookstore.

MAVIS In a *what?*

SIDNEY He works in a bookstore. Part time. (*Almost break-
ing up now*) And as a matter of fact he used to be a communist. (*His sister-in-law just stares at him with an open
mouth and then looks to her sister; she then exhales a
breath to demonstrate she feels that anything is possible
here*) But it's all right, Mav. He's strictly an NMSH-type
Red.

MAVIS What kind is that?

SIDNEY (*Mugging*) "No-more-since-Hungary."

MAVIS Does he know what—ah . . .

SIDNEY Does he know what Gloria does for a living? No.
She told him the model bit.

MAVIS (*Hopefully*) Listen, people like that, I mean com-
munists and things—they're supposed to be very *radical*
. . . about things . . . well . . . (*Pathetically*) Well, aren't
they?

SIDNEY Who can say? There's "people like that" and
"people like that."

MAVIS Is he good-looking? What about Gloria? What does
she . . . ?

SIDNEY (*Deliberately playing it*) Uh, Mavis—

MAVIS I knew this nightmare would have to end . . . It was
just something that happened. It's the way the world is . . .

SIDNEY   He's also a Negro one, Mavis.

MAVIS   ... these days. People don't know what to do with— (*Deep, guttural*) A Negro what—?

SIDNEY (*Still deliberately*)   A Negro communist. That is to say, that he's not a communist any more—but he's still a Negro.

MAVIS (*Looking from one to the other in open-mouthed silence*) Are you— (*A beat, as she turns her head back and forth again*) Are you— (*Finally, composing herself, she crosses to* SIDNEY) sitting there talking about . . . a *colored* boy?

SIDNEY (*Rapidly, wagging his finger*)   1964, Mavis, 1964! "Uncommitted Nations," "Free World!" Don't say it, honey, don't say it! We'll think you're not chic!

MAVIS   I don't think you're funny worth a damn! (*Looking from one to the other*) What do you think Gloria *is?!* (*The question hangs*) If this is your idea of some kind of bohemian joke I just don't think it's cute or clever or *anything*. I would rather see her—

SIDNEY (*Finishing it for her*)   —go on shacking up with any poor sick bastard in the world with a hundred bucks for a convention weekend!
        (*They glare at one another*)

MAVIS   Well now, listen, there are other men in the world! The last time I looked around me there were still some white men left in this world. Some fine ordinary upstanding plain decent very white men who were still looking to marry very white women . . .
        (*During the above* DAVID RAGIN *has descended the*

stairway from his apartment overhead; now he pushes open the door and saunters in. An intense, slim, studied young man, of the latest fashionably casual dress and style, his mannerisms intend to suggest the entirely unmannered—but by choice. He is not in the least—"swish")

IRIS Why hello, David, this is my sister, Mrs. Bryson.

MAVIS How do you do.
(*He sits*)

IRIS (*Facetiously, to him*) I wouldn't bother, but she is from uptown where people knock on doors and all that jazz.

DAVID (*He ignores* MAVIS *completely—wearily*) You have any paper?

IRIS The desk in the bedroom. (DAVID *exits into the bedroom*) David is a playwright who lives upstairs. And we are the government—and we subsidize him.
(MAVIS *nods and turns to* SIDNEY)

MAVIS Well, *he's* sort of cute. Is he married?

SIDNEY (*Simply*) David's gay. (MAVIS *doesn't get it*) Queer. (*Still doesn't*) Homosexual. (*Gets it, drawing back*) Utterly.

MAVIS Oh. (*Afterthought*) Well, maybe she would want a rest . . . (DAVID *re-enters, crosses to the bar for a drink.* MAVIS *gathers up her things*) Well, I should get on. I've got to meet Fred. Did I tell you the news, Iris? Fred's been put in charge of the Folk River Dam Project. Now, what do you think of that?
(SIDNEY *is struck by this*)

IRIS   I think we are a talented family, obviously. Success in whatever we put our— (*Holding—to outrage the sister*) hands to.

MAVIS   Iris, not in front of people.

IRIS   David isn't people. He's a writer. And he worships prostitutes. He says they are the only *real* women—the core of life, as it were. Don't you, David?

MAVIS   The only thing about your flippancies, Iris, is that they don't solve any problems.

SIDNEY   (*Who has remained preoccupied by the earlier remark*) So old Fred is really doing all right for himself, huh?
      (IRIS *lifts her eyes at this knowingly*)

IRIS   Look out, Mavis, you're about to be tapped—

SIDNEY   You!

MAVIS   (*Pleasantly*)   Now Sidney, you know Fred won't invest in a night club.

IRIS   The night club is dead. Long live the newspaper.

SIDNEY   (*To* IRIS)   It wasn't a *night club.*

MAVIS   A newspaper? (*Great intake of breath and, immediately, maternal exhalation*) Oh, Sidney, Sidney, Sidney! You're thirty-seven years old. When are you going to grow up. (*Shaking her head*) A *newspaper.*

SIDNEY   (*Tightly*)   And what would a really "grown-up man" be doing with himself—in your enlightened opinion, Mavis?

MAVIS Well, now, I know for a fact that your brother Manny has offered any number of times to get you a place in his firm. You're very lucky to have a brother in that kind of position, Sidney. A man like Fred had to do it all the hard way. I mean the *hard* way.

SIDNEY And what will happen, Mavis, if I try, knowing better before I even open my mouth, to explain to you—that I consider my brother Manny a failure? I consider Fred a failure. I consider them to be men who accepted the alternatives that circumscribed them when they were born. I don't! I have a different set of alternatives—alternatives that I create! I either want to run my newspaper or —or go be an ambulance driver in Angola. I do not, for any reason, want to become part of the DD and F company.

MAVIS (*Blinking, having heard nothing after "Angola"*) Be an ambulance driver—*where,* dear?

IRIS But, Sidney, you can hardly drive . . .

SIDNEY Oh, forget it!

IRIS (*Hands on hips—to* DAVID) Talk about *bad* Hemingway.

MAVIS Well, I really must go. (*To her sister, softly*) You will let me know when Gloria is coming?

IRIS (*A great sigh*) Mavis—sooner or later you are going to have to learn that Gloria is living her life and doesn't want you to play Mama. Live and let live, that's all.

MAVIS That's just a shoddy little way of trying to avoid responsibility in the world.

SIDNEY   Mavis—please go. It makes me *nervous* to be on your side! (*Bellowing*) ✓

MAVIS   (*To* DAVID, *as she pulls on her gloves*)   What are you writing, young man?

DAVID   Nothing you'd be interested in.

SIDNEY   Go on and tell her about your play, David. There is nothing else she can hear that's shocking today.

DAVID   Cool it, Sidney.

SIDNEY   David is engaged in the supreme effort of trying to wrest the theatre from the stranglehold of Ibsenesque naturalism, are you not, David? (DAVID *just stares indifferently at both of them. He is above, he feels, such repartee*) As a matter of fact he has a play in production right now.

MAVIS   Oh, how nice! Is there something in it for Iris?

IRIS   You're not supposed to do that, Mavis.

SIDNEY   Besides, there are only two characters in David's play and they are both male and married to each other and the entire action takes place in a refrigerator.

MAVIS   (*Eyeing* DAVID *coolly and edging off a little*)   I see.

DAVID   I didn't try to tell you what it was about. (*He has wandered to the sign. He studies it and turns to* SIDNEY, *shaking his head*) And what have you got against the "machine" this week?

SIDNEY   Didn't you ever read *Huckleberry Finn*, David?

IRIS   (*Setting out the supper dishes; indicating her husband*) He's Huck this week.

SIDNEY (*Shouting: raspy-voiced, affecting Hal Holbrook affecting the garrulous old man of conscience*) And therefore "continually happy"! It's a machine, David! With a boss! A highly entrenched boss. Don't believe in bosses. Believe in independent men, like old Huckleberry!

DAVID (*Shaking his head*) That's what I thought. Sidney, don't you know yet "the good guys" and "the bad guys" went out with World War Two?

MAVIS Well, sure. When you come right down to it, one politician *is* just like another.

SIDNEY (*Rocking with his hands in prayerful fashion*) And a new religion is upon the West and it has only one hymn: (*Intoning a mock Mass*) "We are all guilty . . . Father Camus, we are all guilty . . . *Ipso facto*, all guilt is equal . . . Therefore we shall in clear conscience abstain from the social act . . . and even the social thought . . ."

DAVID (*Glaring at him*) Go ahead: kid it. It's easier to kid it than face the pain in it.

SIDNEY (*Possessed by an all-consuming vision of the omnipotent catchword*) Ah, "Pain!" "Pain" in recognizing those dark tunnels which lead back to our primate souls, groveling about—(*He rises to a half-stoop, arms dangling; and ape-like throughout this speech, he crosses to, and up onto, the coffee table and then the sofa*) in caves of sloth. The savage soul of man from whence sprang, in the first place, the Lord of the Flies, Beezlebub himself! (*Rather shouting*) Man, dark gutted creature of ancestral— (*Leaping over the back of the sofa and lifting his hands in Bela Lugosi style*) cannibalism and mysterious all-consuming eeevil! Ahhhhhh. (*Through the bars of the*

59

*rocking chair he snarls and claws at all of them to bur-
lesque this philosophy)* Yahhhh! The Shadow knows.

MAVIS   I just said to Fred this morning: "Say what you like,
it's always something different down at Iris and Sid's."

DAVID *(A little roused finally)*   Well, what is the virtue of
getting one boss out and putting another one in?

SIDNEY   The virtue—the virtue, my dear boy, if you will
pardon the rhetoric, is to participate in some expression
of the people about the way things are, that's all.

DAVID *(Waving around, with derision)*   Well, hel-lo, out
there! *(He shakes his head)* Well, that's what comes from
reading too much Shaw.

SIDNEY *(Angry)*   Yah, well. Speaking of the drama, David,
what *is* your play about?

DAVID   You read it. You tell me.

SIDNEY   No, you tell *me.*

DAVID   It's not for me to say.

SIDNEY *(For him)*   ". . . each person will get from it what
he brings to it?" Right?

DAVID *(As befits the present circumstance)*   To be real
simple-minded about it—yes.

SIDNEY   Then tell me this: What makes *you* the artist and
the *audience* the consumer if they have to write your play
for you?

DAVID   *I* know what it's about. *(SIDNEY merely looks at
him—querulously)* I told you, my plays have to speak for
themselves.

SIDNEY But to *whom*? For *whom*? For whom are they written, and, above all, *why* are they written?

DAVID (*Getting up; his host is beyond belief*) You hate my kind of writing because it goes beyond the walls of Ibsen's prisons and Shaw's lectures—that's *your* problem, Sid.

MAVIS (*Who has been turning from one to the other throughout, fascinated, incredulous, and trying all the while to get a word in edgewise herself*) I just don't know whatever happened to simple people with simple problems in literature.

SIDNEY (*Riding right over her. To* DAVID, *grandiosely*) Oh come now, don't just choose the members of my team that you feel are most vulnerable. Go for my stars, too, David. Or are you afraid to tackle the masks of Euripedes and the shadows and hymns of Shakespeare?
(*They are almost toe to toe*)

DAVID Are you retreating from Ibsen and Shaw?

SIDNEY *Not* on your life! But are you retreating before Euripedes and Shakespeare?

IRIS I get so tired of this endless chess game!

DAVID (*Heading for the door*) All I can say is that I write because I have to and what I have to. You don't know anything about it. Whatever you think of it, Sidney, I write. I squeeze out my own juices and offer them up. I may be afraid, but I write. (ALTON *re-enters with paper bags and the flowers*) Well, Dr. Castro, I presume.

ALTON (*In kind*) Jean Genet, as I live and breathe.
(*They shake hands*)

SIDNEY (*Taking the beer*) Did you bottle it yourself?

IRIS (*Taking her flowers, and exchanging glances with her husband about what they are setting up*) David, are you going to stay to eat?

DAVID Why not?

IRIS (*As they sit down to eat*) Mav?

MAVIS No—dear! I've got to meet Fred.
(*Reluctantly; her matchmaker eyes have not left* ALTON *since his entrance*)

IRIS Alton, I'd like you to meet my sister Mavis. Mavis, this is Alton Scales.

MAVIS How do you do.

ALTON How do you do.
(*As he crosses, she stands admiring him*)

MAVIS (*To* SIDNEY) Is he married?

SIDNEY No.

MAVIS He isn't—ahhh—(*Meaning homosexual*)

SIDNEY We're not sure yet!

MAVIS (*A trill in her voice*) Good night, Mr. Scales.

ALTON Good night.

SIDNEY (*With deliberate casualness*) Oh, Mavis, this is the chap we were just telling you about. (*She looks blank*) From the bookstore.
(*There is silence; all except* DAVID *know the meaning of the moment for* MAVIS. *They variously concentrate*)

IRIS (*Closing the door*) Well, that was some dinner party, thank you. What's with you lately, Sidney? Why do you have to pick at everybody? Where did you get the idea it was up to you to improve everybody? Leave people the hell alone!

SIDNEY (*In a fierce mood*) I don't try to improve people. Or, at least, you can't tell it by you.

IRIS (*Properly hurt*) All right, Sid, one of these days you've got to decide who you want—Margaret Mead or Barbry Allen! I won't play both! As a matter of fact it's getting pretty clear—that I've got to decide too. (*Under her breath, to herself*) God, have I got to decide!

SIDNEY The least excuse and you haul up the old self-pitying introspection bit.

IRIS (*Through her teeth*) What makes you think anybody can live with your insults?

SIDNEY The world needs insults!

IRIS (*The last straw*) Sweet Heaven.
(*She starts to clear the table*)

SIDNEY (*Turning and noticing her exasperation with him*) I'm sorry. (*He moves to help; she rejects this. Several beats*) There's a rally. You wanna go?

IRIS I told you, don't expect me to get involved with that stuff!

SIDNEY All right, all right. You wanna go over to the Black Knight and have a couple of beers?

IRIS No, I don't want to go over to the Black Knight and have a couple of beers.

SIDNEY Well then, suppose *you* just come up with *something, anything* that you would like to do. It will be your first achievement in this entire marriage.

IRIS What does it do for you, Sid? Picking at me like that. Look, why don't you just go to your rally? And leave poor old Iris alone.
(*She turns on the phonograph*)

SIDNEY (*Grabs his jacket and heads for the door; then halts, hand on the knob, flings his jacket to the floor—helpless. More to himself than her:*) Leave "poor old Iris alone"— and watch her turn quietly and willingly into a vegetable.
(IRIS *sits on the window seat, looking off, into the street—as a haunting guitar cuts the silence*)

IRIS (*Softly, fighting back tears*) It's getting different, Sidney, our fighting. Something's either gone out of it or come into it. I don't know which. But it's something that keeps me from wanting to make up with you a few hours later. That's bad, isn't it?

SIDNEY Yeah, that's bad.
(*He turns and looks at his wife; she is crying—then picks up his jacket and starts out*)

IRIS (*Crying out*) Then let's put up a fight for it, Sidney! I mean it—let's fight like hell for it.
(*He halts at the outer staircase and stands clutching the rail and looking back toward the room where his wife sits looking after him, as the light fades on all but the two of them and the voice of Joan Baez, singing "All My Trials," fills the darkening stage*)

Act Two

Scene One

Time: Just before daybreak. The following day.

At rise: Only the faint light of pre-dawn illumines the out-side staircase landing over the BRUSTEIN *doorway; here* SID-NEY *lies, on his back, arms underhead, one leg doubled up and the other resting on his knee. New York at this hour is a world known to few of its inhabitants, and the silence of the great sleeping city is only accentuated by its few familiar sounds: the occasional moan of a foghorn on the Hudson or, now and then, the whirr of tires or clatter of a milk truck. The apartment is dark.*

Presently SIDNEY *sits up, picks up his banjo and, legs dangling over the patio, begins to pick it. The melody seems surely drawn from that other world which ever beckons him, a wistful, throbbing mountain blues. As he plays the lighting shifts magically, and nonrealistically, to create the mountain of his dreams. Gone is even the distant foghorn; he is no longer in the city. After several phrases of this, the music soars and quickens into a vibrant, stinging hoedown and the* IRIS-*of-his-Mind appears, barefooted, with flowing hair and mountain dress, and mounts the steps. She embraces him and then, as by the lore of hill people, is possessed by these rhythms, and dances in the shadows before him. The dance is a moving montage of all the bits and pieces of dance Americana: the dip for the oyster, the grand right and left.* SIDNEY'S *banjo drives her on until both these spirits are ex-hausted and the mountain nymph gives him a final kiss and*

71

flees. He sits on, spent, plucks idly at the instrument. Now a light appears in the apartment's bedroom doorway and his wife enters through it, belting her robe, yawning, rubbing her eyes.

IRIS   Sid—? (*He does not reply or even hear her*) Sidney? (*She switches on the lamp. For a moment stands blankly, then goes to the door and leans out*)   What are you doing up there? You'll wake the neighbors.

SIDNEY (*In the same unbroken reverie*)   They can't hear me, Iris.

IRIS (*At the foot of the steps*)   Oh, Sidney, you're a nut. C'mon down, I'll make you some coffee.
            (*She fishes out her cigarettes and lights one*)

SIDNEY (*Shakes his head*)   Listen! Do you hear the brook? There is nothing like clear brook water at daybreak. And when you drink, it gives back your own image.

IRIS (*Charmed in spite of herself*)   You'll catch cold, Sidney. It's too early for games. Come to bed.

SIDNEY   No, Iris. Come up. (*She does, as he speaks; and, finally, kneels beside him*) Look at the pines—look at the goddamn pines. You can taste and feel the scent of them. And if you look down, down through the mist, you will make out the thin line of dawn far distant. There's not another soul for miles, and if you listen, *really* listen—you might almost hear yourself think.

IRIS (*Surveying the realm, gently laughing*)   This is some mountain.

SIDNEY (*Playful proprietary pride*)   It's a small mountain —but it's ours.

IRIS   Sidney . . . how much is fourteen and fourteen?
(*She smiles and touches his face—and, for the moment, enters fully into his dream*)

SIDNEY (*Fondling her hair*)   "Nymph in . . . all . . . my Orisons remembered."

IRIS (*Looking up at him thoughtfully*)   It really gets to you, doesn't it? Being here. You really are happy? You'd like to live right here, in the woods, wouldn't you?

SIDNEY   Yes. Yes. I would.

IRIS   And you're afraid to ask me to do something like that, aren't you? (*No answer*) Afraid I'll look around at the woods and the brook and say, "*Here? Live?*" (*They both laugh at her mugging of her own attitude*) And the worst of it is you'd be right. I would say exactly that. I wouldn't want to live here. (*Drooping her head a bit*) I'm sorry. The truth is that I am cold and bored. I feel like watching television. I feel like having a swinging argument. I feel like sitting in a stupid movie or, or even a night club, a real stupid night club with dirty jokes and bad dancers. (*Looking at him*) I've changed on you, haven't I, Sid? This particular mountain girl has been turning into an urban wastelander. (*Rather sweetly, still looking at him*) Sorry. (*Several beats, she has been thinking of this*) Most of all, I hate my hair. (*A beat*) The things you don't know about me! (*A little laugh*) Did you know, for instance, that you're the reason I wear it like this in the first place? (*Shaking her head with the little laugh again*) There's a different style of "man trap" in every kind of woman. When I first came here, you know, I was working, dancing in this funny little old nothing of a sawed-off

73

club, you know. And like I thought that the men who came there were not the ones that I came to the (*Charade-style quote marks*) big city—to meet. I mean they were the kind that you could meet back home. So one of the girls who worked there and knew all the this-and-that listened to me and she said, "Well, honey, if that's what you're looking for, you've gotta go down to the Black Knight Tavern and sit." (*Smiling*) "Let your hair grow and go down to the Black Knight Tavern." Sounds like a folk song. Well, anyhow, the fourth time I went there, remember, it was about to . . . here. (*Marking off the shorter place*) And there you were, just like that, sitting in that corner booth with—(*Remembering*) Marty and Alt, wasn't it? Yes, it was Marty and Alt. And there you were sitting there, "holding forth." And I said to m'self: There's the one. After that I started eating vitamins to make m'hair grow faster. (*He laughs a soft, delighted "Oh, Iris!"*) So, s'help me! It's true! This same girl who told me everything, she got these vitamins for me too. And, well— *something* worked.

SIDNEY I'm charmed.

IRIS Women are a mess, aren't they? I mean they get these *fantastic* IDEAS about things, I· mean life and all, when they're like three, you know. And nothing, I mean nothing gets it out of you. When I got off that train from Trenersville ten years ago I knew one thing in this world: I wanted to meet men who were as—as different from Papa as—as possible.

SIDNEY (*Taking her hand*) Listen, Iris. Listen to the woods. Let's go for a walk.

IRIS (*Huddling close*) It's too cold. And dark. And the woods frighten me.

SIDNEY   All right then, let's just go into the cabin and I'll make us a bang-up fire and some of the hottest coffee ever brewed. (*She just looks at him*) You just want to go back to the city, don't you?

IRIS   Yes.

SIDNEY   You really hate it here?

IRIS   Yes. (*The tears come; tears of frustration, as she does not know exactly why. Gesturing around*) I was born in country like this, you know, the real thing. I mean you didn't drive out anywhere to sort of *see* it. You just sat down on the back porch and—there it was. Something to run from; something to get the hell away from as fast as you could. All of us felt like that, me, Mav—Gloria.

SIDNEY   Then you've always hated coming here. I didn't know that.

IRIS (*Sort of a painful whine born of the effort to really make him finally understand*)   No, I didn't *always* hate it . . . the first couple of years I just wanted to do what you wanted to do, be where you were—you know, sort of wild and romantic the way it was supposed to be—(*A great burst of frustration*) I mean, I thought it was going to be different. Papa was so crude and stupid . . . You know, I never heard my father make an abstract thought in his life; and, well, he had plenty of time to think, if you know what I mean. Didn't work that steady. And each of us; I think we've sort of grown up wanting some part of Papa that we thought was the thing missing in him. I wanted somebody who could, well, think; Mavis wanted some-body steady and ordinary. And Gloria, well, you know— rich men. Lots of them. (*Lifting up her hand anticipat-ing*) I know you're going to tell me that's parlor analysis, and it is, but—

SIDNEY I'm not saying anything, Iris. I'm listening. I really am. I am listening to you.

IRIS And now something is happening to me, changing me. Since we've been married. Sometimes, Sidney, I think if—if I hear any more talk from Alton and Max and David and—you—I'll shrivel up and die from it. You know what I want, Sidney? I am twenty-nine and I want to begin to know that when I die more than ten or a hundred people will know the difference. I want to *make* it, Sid. *Whatever* that means and *however* it means it: That's what I want. (*He is nodding; he genuinely under-stands and is deeply pained by it*) Anyhow, what does it do for you, Sid? To come up here and talk to your—what do you call them—

SIDNEY (*Smilingly*) My trolls.

IRIS Yeah. 'Cause I tried having a few words with 'em and like what they had to say to me was nothing.

SIDNEY (*Looking around*) Coming here makes me believe that the planet is mine again. In the primeval sense. Man and earth and earth and man and all that. You know. That we have just been born, the earth and me, and are just starting out. There is no pollution, no hurt; just me and this ball of minerals and gases suddenly shot together out of the cosmos.

IRIS (*Looking at him, head tilted puppy style, mouth ajar*)
Jeees.

SIDNEY   I love you very much.
> (*They are quiet; he lifts his banjo and plays a little.
> Then it is still. After a long beat:*)

IRIS   Take me back to the city, please, Sid.
> (*He gets up and puts his banjo over his shoulder and
> takes her hand and they start down the steps—while
> at the same time the magic that is* SIDNEY'*s World
> fades and the lighting returns to normal. A passing
> truck guns its motor and day breaks on the city*)

IRIS (*At the foot of the steps. Remembering*)   Sidney, it's
Tuesday: you've got to move the car!
> (*They start to go in*)

Dimout

SCENE TWO

Time: An evening in late summer.

*In the darkness—and in sharp contrast to the prior mood
—a soundtruck loudspeaker blares out the buoyant, boister-
ous strains of "The Wally O'Hara Campaign Song"—sung
by a folk group to the accompaniment of booming guitars
and the occasional cheers and comments of the crowd, which
joins in on the chorus.*

THE WALLY O'HARA CAMPAIGN SONG

Sing out the old, sing in the new,
It's your ballot and it's got a lot of work to do;
Sing out the old, sing in the new,
Wally O'Hara is the man for you!

CHORUS Wally O'Hara, Wally O'Hara
      Wally O'Hara is the man—for—you!

Sweep out the old, sweep in the new,
We've got a lot of sweeping to do;
Sweep out the old, sweep in the new,
Wally O'Hara is the man for you!

CHORUS (*Repeats*)
      Who knows the people, every one?
      (Wally! Wally!)
      Who knows the job that must be done?
      (Wally! Wally!)

78

Who is the man to beat the machine?
Who'll clean up this district and keep it clean?
(Wally! Wal-ly O'Hara!)

Vote out the old, vote in the new,
It's your ballot and it's got a lot of work to do;
Vote out the old, vote in the new,
Wally O'Hara is the man for you!

CHORUS (*Repeats*)

The song is not performed for its own sake, but rather as it might be by local talent from a touring vehicle in the campaign's heat; and, inevitably too, the speaker system is overworked, with resultant static and crackle from time to time. Still, what is lacking in polish is more than made up in fervor, and the tone is festive. The song should not be heard in its entirety, but gained in and out as indicated at appropriate moments. As the lights come up SIDNEY *and* WALLY *come on from the right in animated conversation. Each carries an armload of leaflets, and* SIDNEY, *a rolled-up flag.* WALLY *has his free arm about* SIDNEY'S *shoulder and is agitated, moist-eyed.* SIDNEY *is more bemused. The sound-truck music moves off in the distance.*

WALLY (*With self-absorbed wonder*)   No, Sid, I mean it. You can feel it in the air. There's a difference this time, a rumbling in the streets. My God, did you see the reception we got on Christopher Street? I tell you we really have underestimated the whole thing. (*Looking out at the audience*) I mean it, we are going to win. Sidney, baby, we are going to win this thing, *I am going to win!*
(*He slaps* SIDNEY *on the back, crosses and exits with the flag*)

79

SIDNEY (*With disbelieving eyes. To the audience*) It's a disease. We are at that point in a campaign which ushers in the dementia of the dark horse. Now comes the delusion, as ancient as elections themselves, which takes over the soul of the candidate. There is nothing to be done about it: it is in the nature of the type. He really thinks he is going to win. (*Whistling the campaign song, he balances his leaflets in the doorway and fishes for his keys —as* DAVID *enters, reading a newspaper and carrying a batch of others. To* DAVID) So?

DAVID (*Dryly, as if above self-appreciation*) "A complete unqualified hit."
    (*He hands* SIDNEY *the paper*)

SIDNEY I'll be damned. Well, congratulations. Come on, I'll give you a drink.
    (*They enter*)

IRIS (*Menacingly, from the bedroom*) Sid? Did you say it was all right for Alton to leave the loudspeaker system in the *bathtub*?

SIDNEY That clown. (*The phone rings. He picks it up*) No, no, no . . . (*Finding it on a wall map of the Village*) You're in the Eighth Election District. (*He hangs up*)

IRIS (*Over part of the above—in a tizzy*) And *who* gave this number as the *canvassing* headquarters? (*Shouting*) I haven't been off the phone all afternoon!

SIDNEY (*To* IRIS, *changing the subject*) Did you see the reviews? We don't have to put on any more. We know a celebrity.

DAVID Will you cut it out.

SIDNEY Just listen—(*He reads aloud*) "... Mr. Ragin has found a device which transcends language itself. In his work all façade fades, all panaceas dissolve, and the ultimate questions are finally asked of existence itself . . ." (*The obvious joke on himself*) See. Just like I always said. (SIDNEY *gives him his drink. They toast.* SIDNEY *looks about the room for something. Then to* IRIS, *ever so sweetly, afraid of rousing the dead*) Oh, Iris, did they leave the mailing piece? We've got all those envelopes to stuff.

IRIS (*Shrieking, a veritable avenging Fury by now*) Sidney, if you don't get that trash out of here *today*, I'm going to *burn* the apartment down!!!
      (SIDNEY *finds the enclosures, stacks them on the table and begins stuffing envelopes, whistling as he does—all but ignoring* DAVID)

DAVID By your recent antics I take it you believe there is something to be affected by all this? Presumably for the good?

SIDNEY (*Not taking the bait, gaily*) C'mon, David. There is work to be done. Lend a hand. (*The phone rings. He answers*) Yes? No, it's *not* a mistake . . . Fourth Street *does* cross Eleventh Street.
      (*He hangs up, goes back to work*)

DAVID (*Studying him as a specimen*) Well, I don't attack you for it. I know it is something most men, even thinking men, resist long after they know better.

SIDNEY (*Between envelopes, not even raising his eyes*) You mean that Zarathustra has spoken—and God is dead?

DAVID   Yes.

SIDNEY   "Progress" is an illusion and the only reality is—
nothing?

DAVID   You surprise me. Can one debate it?

SIDNEY   (*Finally sitting back for this; he feels himself in fine fettle*)   One can observe that it is the debate which is, for all human purposes, beside the point. The *debate* which is absurd. The "why" of why we are here is an intrigue for adolescents; the "how" is what must command the living. Which is why I have lately become an insurgent again.
(*Back to work. The phone rings again—and this time* IRIS *comes shrieking out of the bedroom: one more call and she* will *burn the apartment down! She wears the dress* MAVIS *bought*)

IRIS   *Sid-nee*—(*Noticing* DAVID *for the first time*) David. (*Genuinely*) My God, those reviews! It's marvelous. How do you feel?

SIDNEY   (*On the phone*)   You don't say? Right . . . right . . . right.

DAVID   (*To* IRIS. *Embarrassed by her display*)   Please. Well, I've got to go to work.

IRIS   Work? Already? Aren't you just going to bask awhile or something?

DAVID (*Sadly*)   Doing what? See you.
(*Exits*)

SIDNEY   (*Hangs up*)   You know what, the craziest thing is happening to Wally . . . that clown is actually—(*As the fact of* MAVIS' *dress dawns on him*) Well, get you!

IRIS   I look pretty all right in this—huh, Sid?

SIDNEY   Sure, if you like the type. I like you in other things better.

IRIS   I know. I'm going out tonight, Sidney.

SIDNEY   Yeah? Where? (*Not thinking about that too much*) You know not one, not one of the entire collection I've surrounded myself with . . .

IRIS   I talked to Lucille Terry today. She's having a cocktail party.

SIDNEY   Lucille Terry? *Lucille Terry!* Where in the name of God did she pop up from? I didn't know that you still saw each other.

IRIS   We haven't in years. But, you know, just like that people suddenly call each other up. So just like that she called me up last week about this party she was having.

SIDNEY   (*His hand on the phone; he couldn't care less*) How is Lucy? Lemme see now, gotta call Mickey Dafoe, put on the old Establishment voice. "Hello, Mr. Dafoe, well, how are you, sir—" Fix me a drink, why doncha, honey?

IRIS   (*Crossing to the pantry; in a muted voice*)   Lucy didn't call me, Sid. I called *her.*

SIDNEY   (*Still thinking more about the call he has to make*) Yeah? You know I really hate to give fuel to Alton's narrow view of the world, but there is turning out to be a surprising amount of validity to his notions of base and superstructure. Two banks, a restaurant and three real

83

estate firms have already canceled ads since we've come out for Wally . . .

IRIS (*Disinterested, bringing him his drink*) Oh, really— (*The phone rings*) Interesting.

SIDNEY (*Picking it up*) Yes, Renee . . . She says what? . . . Sure, O'Hara could be an Italian name. . . Or his *mother's* Italian. (*Hangs up, to* IRIS) Well, she *could* be. (*Noticing her standing there, finally just looking at him quietly*) Aw, I'm sorry, honey, I really am, but I just don't feel like going to any party tonight. Especially the uptown scene. Not tonight. (*He is taking the entire situation lightly*) Tell Lucy we love her but no.

IRIS (*Starkly, staring down at him*) I wasn't asking you to come with me, Sidney.
> (*He drinks, slowly absorbs this last remark and, for the first time, reacts with some sense of the portentousness of the moment*)

SIDNEY Oh?

IRIS That's sort of the point. I—I am going alone.

SIDNEY Oh. (*They are both quiet; neither looking at the other; the awkwardness shouts*) Well, hell, so you're going to a party. Great. You should do things alone sometimes. Everybody should. What are we acting so funny about it for?

IRIS Because we know it isn't just *a* party. It's the fact that I want to go. That I called Lucy.

SIDNEY (*Very worried*) Well, don't worry about it. It's okay. Just have a nice time, that's all.

IRIS (*Sadly*) Would you—would you like me to make you some supper before I go?

SIDNEY (*Rising and crossing away not to face her*) Uh—no. No. Thanks. Wally and I are due on MacDougal Street in an hour. We'll go out with the kids after or something.

IRIS You could have them here. There's—there's a lot of stuff in the box and—plenty of beer.

SIDNEY (*Getting it fully*) Is there?

IRIS Yes. I'm sorry, Sid.

SIDNEY You're planning on being late, aren't you?

IRIS I think it'll be kind of late.

SIDNEY (*Finally*) Who's going to be at this party, Iris?

IRIS How do I know who's going to be there? Lucy's friends.

SIDNEY Lucy's friends. The "would-be" set, as I recall it.

IRIS Huh?

SIDNEY The "would-be" set, would-be actresses, would-be producers. The would-bes tend to collect around Lucy a lot.

IRIS Some of her friends are pretty successful.

SIDNEY Like Ben Asch?
(*She wheels and they exchange a violent conversation without words*)

IRIS (*Getting into her shoes*) Look, Sid; let's make an agreement based on the recognition of reality. The reality

85

being that the big thaw has set in with us and that we don't know what that means yet. So let's make some real civilized kind of agreement that until—well—until we know just what we feel, I mean about everything—let's not ask each other a whole lot of slimy questions.

SIDNEY I'll ask all the slimy questions I want! Listen, Iris, have you been seeing this clown or something?

IRIS Only once—after the time I told you.

SIDNEY Once is all it takes.

IRIS He thinks he can help me.

SIDNEY Do what?

IRIS Break in, that's what!

SIDNEY Then why didn't he see *us?*

IRIS I don't know, Sidney. I guess he was under the impression that I was a big girl now.

SIDNEY I'll bet!

IRIS But none of this is the main point, Sid. The main point is that I feel I want to do something else with my life. Other than—

SIDNEY Other than what?

IRIS Other than—this. Other than conversation about the Reformation; other than conversations about Albert Camus. Other than scraping together enough pancake money to study with every has-been actor who's teaching now because he can't work any more. There has to be another way.

SIDNEY From the has-beens to the would-bes. I'll admit there is a progression there!

IRIS Ben knows some extremely influential people. People who have been around—people who *do* the things they mean to do.

SIDNEY Where?

IRIS In the theatre and in politics too! Especially in politics. People who are not just talkers—but doers. Who do not take on a newspaper they cannot even afford and then run it into the ground for a hopeless campaign. And for what? For Wally? If even half of what they say about Wally is true—

SIDNEY Oh? And just what do "they" say?
    (*He waits, knowing as he does, there is nothing she can say*)

IRIS (*Trapped*) Well, I don't know about any of this, but Lucy thinks—

SIDNEY (*Holding up one hand; the issue is closed*) Right the first time, Iris! You *don't* know.

IRIS Sidney, this is not the Silver Dagger you're getting into. These people are sharks.

SIDNEY (*With finality; father knows best*) Look, Iris, I'll make a deal with you: You let me fight City Hall and I'll stay out of Shubert Alley.

IRIS (*Quietly; she has had it*) All right, Sidney.

87

SIDNEY   And stop ducking the main point: What is this glorious doer Ben Asch going to do for you?

IRIS   As a matter of fact he's already got me some work.

SIDNEY   Oh—why haven't you mentioned it? What show?

IRIS (*Defensively*)   It isn't exactly a show—but it is acting. Sort of. (*He stares at her*) It's a TV commercial . . .

SIDNEY (*Laughing*)   Oh, Iris, Iris.

IRIS (*Hotly*)   Oh, aren't we better than everybody, Sidney Brustein! Aren't we above it! Well, I have news: If he gets me that job, I am going to take it. And when I'm doing it—I'll know that it beats hell out of slinging hash while I wait for "pure art" to come along.

SIDNEY   Iris, it's not just the *what* you're getting into—it's the *how*. You've got no business hanging out with Lucy and that crowd. How can it be that after five years of life with me you don't know better than this?
     (*He has taken hold of her*)

IRIS (*Exploding, near tears*)   I have learned *a lot* after five years of life with you, Sidney! When I met you I thought Kant was a stilted way of saying cannot; I thought Puccini was a kind of spaghetti; I thought the louder an actor yelled and fell out on the floor the greater he was. But you taught me to look deeper and harder. At everything: from Japanese painting to acting. Including, Sidney, my *own* acting. Thanks to you, I now know something I wouldn't have learned if it hadn't been for you. The fact . . . the *fact* that I am probably the world's *lousiest* actress . . . (*He releases her*) So, there it is, the trouble with looking at ourselves honestly, Sidney, is that we come up with the truth. And, baby, the truth is a bitch.

(*Iris goes out the door*)

SIDNEY (*Going after her*) Iris, Iris, just listen—

IRIS (*Facing him. Resolutely; she will not be stopped*) All I know is that, from now on, I just want something to happen in my life. I don't much care *what*. Just something.

SIDNEY I just want you to know that—whatever happens— you've been one of the few things in my life that made me happy.

IRIS (*An anguished voice—for* both *of them*) Oh, Sid, "happy." (*She reaches up, to touch his face a moment*) Whoever started that anyhow? What little bastard was it? Teaching little kids there was such a thing?

> (*She exits.* SIDNEY *goes back inside, sits, goes to the drawing board, then leaves that and picks up his banjo and then, with resolution, steps to the door and throws it open*)

SIDNEY Hey—David . . . David! Can you come down a sec—

> (*But* DAVID *is right there, on his way out—rather sheepish, more boyish, genuine than in his prior scenes*)

DAVID (*A grin*) Oh, you caught me. Waaaal, I decided to go out after all. Maybe I owe myself, under the circumstances, at least one night off. (*He continues, halts, comes back.* SIDNEY *hardly hears him; he is thinking of something intently*) I'll tell you the truth . . . It—it seemed emptier than usual up there. I swore I wouldn't, you know—(*Embarrassed at the humanity of his present feelings*) sort of go out and strut around . . . But by God, it's almost like I *have* to. Do you know what I mean? I I mean—(*He laughs freely and drops his hands*) I mean I *feel pretty good.*

SIDNEY (*Half steering, half pushing him inside*) Well, why not! Who wouldn't? . . . C'mon in a sec . . .

DAVID (*Suddenly, not aware that he is mainly talking to himself under the circumstances*) Don't make fun of me, Sidney! The truth is, today is not yesterday. Nothing could have made me believe this yesterday— But I am somebody else today. Inside. It's in my rooms upstairs, it's in my coat . . . it's in my skin. Christ, Sid—(*Pure unadulterated wonder*) I'm famous. (*A grin*) I have to go outside and find out what it's like to wear it in the streets. (*Sobering*) As if I can't guess. Everybody will just be more self-conscious, phonier than they would have been yesterday. Just because my picture was in the papers. It's crazy. The phone keeps on ringing. For years I made fun of people who had unlisted numbers. First thing Monday— I'll have to get one. (*Final smile*) G'night, Sid.

SIDNEY No, wait a minute. Please. I'd like to talk to you. You want a drink?

DAVID What do you want, Sidney? I'm in a hurry!

SIDNEY (*Not looking at him*) Hey—David . . . it's as good as on, isn't it?

DAVID (*Turning*) What—?

SIDNEY (*A little madly*) Your next play. It's as good as on —isn't it? Every producer in town will be looking for it, won't they?

DAVID (*Annoyed to talk about this; a modest person in the true sense*) Well . . . my agent said there've been some calls already—(*A sigh about producers*) First you can't get into their offices—

SIDNEY You're very talented, David.

DAVID I have to go.
(*He turns on his heels to leave*)

SIDNEY No. Look, remember we went once, together, to see that thing that Iris was in a couple of years ago?

DAVID Yes?

SIDNEY Well, you thought she was pretty good. Even better than I thought she was, didn't you? You said so.

DAVID Those were my polite years. When I still cared what people thought about me.

SIDNEY No, come on, you said that you thought what she did was pretty good.

DAVID When she just danced. When she spoke, when she had lines, it was horrible.

SIDNEY Well, now, *not horrible*. Just average.

DAVID What do you want, Sidney?

SIDNEY She's a hung-up kid, David. She needs something to happen for her, before she gets all turned around sideways.

DAVID (*Unrelentingly*)   What is it that you want, Sidney?

SIDNEY (*Sitting and turning away from the other man*) Write her into your play, David. Something for her. Something simple that she can do. With dancing.

DAVID (*Absorbing it; pressing his lips together with sadness and pulling his collar up about his ears*)   I have to go now, Sid.

SIDNEY   It wouldn't have to be a big part, for Christ's sake! Look, she *needs* something to happen for her, don't you understand?

DAVID   You solve your marriage problems any way you have to, Sidney. I won't judge you, but don't bring them to me.

SIDNEY   I'll do the review—
    (*Catching* DAVID *in the door,* SIDNEY *stops himself, amazed at the thought*)

DAVID (*Turning slowly back to him*)   What did you say? (SIDNEY *is quiet, knowing the enormity of his error*) Okay, I'll pretend I never heard you. I am going out now, Sidney. I don't need to experience the other part of this scene. The recovery of Morality and all that. That's *up*-town drama. I can't stand those. I'll go and let you have this one all by yourself.
    (*He starts out again, fast.* SIDNEY *grabs him*)

SIDNEY   What's so awful about it? Can't you write about more than two characters at a time? How could it hurt?

DAVID   Just in case you don't understand me at all, Sidney, I'll tell you something. Prostitutes interest me clinically; I've not the least intention of ever becoming one. (*Cross-*

ing close to SIDNEY *so that they are face to face*) Now I'll tell you something else. Look into this cynic's eyes, Sidney. Go ahead, look! And finally understand what these pools of implacable cynicism stand for! It's integrity, Sidney.

SIDNEY (*In profound humiliation*) Don't feel so holy about it, David. I asked and you refused. Let's forget it. It was such a little—such a tiny little act on the part of a slightly desperate man.

DAVID Such a tiny little corruption. Not three people in the whole world would ever really care whether or not my little insignificant play did or did not have its unities stretched to just happen to include a part for your wife in trade for a patch of glowing praise in your paper. Not three people in the whole world. That's the magic of the tiny corruptions, isn't it, Sidney? Their insignificance makes them so appealing.

SIDNEY (*Profoundly embarrassed*) All right. I asked and you refused. Let's forget it.

DAVID (*All warmth has receded; his voice is tight, harsh and cold*) Well, thanks for something, anyway. I was really too mellow to go out in this world. Too vulnerable. I would have been torn to pieces. But you've fixed that. I'm ready for it now.

(WALLY *has crossed outside and enters in high jubilance, doing minstrel kicks, wiggling his hat above his head*)

WALLY (*Singing, clowning*)
"When the red, red, robin
Comes bob, bob, bobbin' along—!"

93

DAVID (*Dryly*) Enter, the future.

WALLY (*Halting the clowning; to* DAVID) Could be, could be. (*Facetiously, flippantly in high spirits*) Allow me to offer the grim Past a leaflet. (*To* SIDNEY) You should have seen the crowd on Hudson Street. Sidney, there is something *happening!*

DAVID (*Demonstratively crumpling the leaflet and letting it fall to the floor*) It is my fondest hope and greatest expectation that one of these days the hoods will just get tired of you children and wrap you up in sacks and drop you in the river as in the old days.

WALLY Well now—(*Nodding up and down, as if to encourage. Facetiously*) There is an utterance from the very bowels of disenchantment. The only problem is, young man, you wear it badly. Those French intellectuals you aim to be imitating have a few things weighing on them that you don't know very much about. Including two world wars and the loss of an empire. What's weighing you down, David? As far as I have ever been able to make out from your writings—some problem or other about your mother?

DAVID Your friend—(*Angry, but not wishing to show it*) is very clever, isn't he, Sidney? (*To* SIDNEY *alone*) Put his remarks alongside the little proposition you just made me and see what you think of my disgust with both of you.
(*He turns and exits*)

WALLY (*Limp-wristedly*) "Well, I hope yew got that!"

SIDNEY Cut it out. He's not swish. (*Dully*) Aside from which, he's right.

94

WALLY   Ah me, ah me: pessimism is weighing heavily on the land. I wonder why. How's Iris?

SIDNEY   Fine.

WALLY   What's happening?

SIDNEY   What do you mean what's happening?

WALLY   She seems to be spending a lot of time lately with the girl friend of one of my poker-playing buddies, that's all.

SIDNEY   If you were married, you'd understand. Things get a little strained . . .

WALLY   Seems like a funny crowd for Iris. (*Noticing suddenly that* SIDNEY *is doubled over with pain*) What's the matter?

SIDNEY   My ulcer is having a rock-and-roll party.

WALLY   Where's your medicine? I'll get it for you.

SIDNEY   In the bathroom. The brown bottle. (*Bitterly*) They're tranquilizers.

WALLY (*Reading from the bottle*)   Says you're supposed to take one every morning. Didn't you take it?

SIDNEY   No.

WALLY   Why not?

SIDNEY   Because I hate them.

WALLY   Don't be such a nut. You should take them. It keeps you from getting upset about every little thing. That's the point of them.
      (*He hands the pills to* SIDNEY, *who is sitting in the rocker*)

SIDNEY (*Turning his head slowly to his friend*) "Every little thing," huh, Wally. (*Reaching out and taking the pill and the water and setting them carefully in front of him on the table*) Yes, by all means hand me the chloroform of my passions; the sweetening of my conscience; the balm of my glands. (*Lifting the pills like Poor Yorick's skull*) Oh blessèd age! That has provided that I need never live again in the full temper of my rage. (*Rising and crossing to drawing board, he picks up a yardstick, which, in his hand, becomes the "sword" of the speech*) In the ancient times, the good men among my ancestors, when they heard of evil, strapped a sword to their loins and strode into the desert; and when they found it, they cut it down—or were cut down and bloodied the earth with purifying death. But how does one confront these thousand nameless faceless vapors that are the evil of our time? Could a sword pierce it? (*Turning his eyes to* WALLY) Look at me, Wally . . . Wrath has become a poisoned gastric juice in the intestine. One does not *smite* evil any more: one holds one's gut, thus—and takes a pill. (*As he rises suddenly to full Jovian stance*) Oh, but to take up the sword of the Maccabeans again! (*He closes down from the mighty gesture and sets down the "sword," then turns and lamely takes his pill and water*) L'chaim!

Quick fadeout

Curtain

Rita Moreno and Gabriel Dell as IRIS BRUSTEIN and SIDNEY BRUSTEIN

Scene Three

Time: Election night. Early fall.

In the darkness, the sounds of a not-too-far-distant victory celebration are heard: shouting, cheers and jubilation, the indistinct electronic mumble of a loudspeaker, and "The Wally O'Hara Campaign Song"—not sung this time by a few, but taken over by the whole crowd. Now and then a distinct shout "Wally!" or "O'Hara" can be heard to cut through.

At rise: SIDNEY *enters, in this spirit, and fumbles for his key in the entrance. The phone rings within. He leaves the door ajar as he crosses to the phone, snatching up glass and bottle en route. The sound dims somewhat but continues under.*

SIDNEY (*Sheer exhilaration; he is heady with victory, not drink*) Oh—waaal, hello, dere, Mr. Dafoe! (*Fumbling with phone and bottle*) Oh, I'm right here. Right here! . . . Yes, yes . . . well, as I'm sure you can understand, we're in no mood to backtrack on anything today, Mr. Dafoe . . . Yes, by God, I am being smug, Mr. Dafoe! Wouldn't you be . . . Don't you realize what happened? Of all the crazy, impossible, illogical . . . Well, it *did* happen. We dead have in fact awakened, Mr. Dafoe! All right then, I will speak to you when I am sober. (*He hangs up and takes the first drink.* ALTON *has entered during the above and has stood quietly with his back to the door waiting for* SIDNEY

97

to finish. SIDNEY *sees him—but not his expression*) Alton, old baby, do you know the main trouble with us believers in this world? *We don't believe!* I didn't believe that what happened today could happen in a million years. That we would win. That little old ladies and big tough truck drivers and little skinny Madison Avenue ad men would all get up today and go out and wipe out the Big Boss in one fell stroke! Can you believe it? (*He sits and savors the wonder, shaking his head back and forth, then drinks again*) You know what? We don't know anything about the human race, that's what. Not a damn thing when you come down to it. (*Suddenly thinking of a good taunt victim*) Where's that David? (*Gets up and goes outside. The cheers and sound come up*) Where is that sad-eyed little bastard today? Twenty years of political history overturned and he goes into hiding. (*Shouting up*) Hey, Strindberg! Where are you? What are you avoiding the partisans for today, huh?

ALTON (*Dully*)   Leave him alone.

SIDNEY   Leave him alone? I am going to make that sophomoric little elf eat his nineteenth-century profundities with a spoon! Do you know what we proved today, Alton? Do you *realize* what we proved? We proved that what the people need, what they want, is alternatives. Give them alternatives and all the dull stupid negative old shibboleths go up in smoke. *Poof!* (ALTON *is out of it; standing forlornly in a concentration of his own, not listening, not hearing*) Look, Alt, do you know how *old* the world is? Not very damn old. Why, the whole frigging planetary system is only five billion years old. By eternity's measure—perhaps one day and one night! Do you get me?

... And, look, it was only twenty-five million years ago that primitive apes were strolling around at a half stoop, you know what I mean, Alt. And they were apes, *not men,* apes. Just apes. (*Just a touch of liquor's fire as well as his own*) By God, this is beautiful! Lucidity is positively flowing over me like the sweet oils of Persia! Apes! And between them and us came all the sub boys: Java, Peking, Neanderthal Man and then finally, a long, long time after, finally: Cro Magnon Man. A mere, a lousy, a nothing of a teensy little thirty thousand years ago. Alton, *he's a baby!* He's an infant!

ALTON (*Lifting bleary eyes wearily*)   Who, Sidney?

SIDNEY   *Man! The human race!* Yesterday he made a wheel, and fire, so today we're all demanding to know why he hasn't made universal beauty and wisdom and truth too! (*Slumping down, spent*) A few thousand lousy years he's had to figure out a calendar, and how to make the corn grow; a few lousy years to figure out—*everything.* And we give 'im hell. (*Lifting his eyes with plaintive joy*) All he needs is a little more time ... and he'll be all right, doncha think, Alt? Time and alternatives, like today? Maybe—maybe we could get through the whole thing then. You think? (*Noting the other's face finally, which is just staring at him*) Were you pulling for the other side or something? (*Then rising and laughing and, lifting up his glass, singing Higgins' song from* My Fair Lady) "I said to him we did it, we did it!" (*Then*) What the hell is the matter with you?

ALTON (*His eyes trained on* SIDNEY)   Is it true, Sid?

SIDNEY (*Knowing at once*)   Is what true—?

ALTON (*Rising*)   We've hung out together a long time; don't crap around. Is it true? Is it true she's a hooker? And you were going to let me marry her? (SIDNEY *says nothing; he sits, exhaling a great troubled sigh*) Why didn't you tell me?

SIDNEY (*Staring at the floor*)   It wasn't my place to do so. It was for Gloria to tell you. People change. She'll change. She needs someone. Just don't make me sick today, Alton. Just don't act like a fraternity boy meeting his own girl under the lamppost.

ALTON   How would you act? (*They stare at one another*) When you go into the mines, Sid, you get coal in your skin; if you're a fisherman, you will reek of fish! . . . She doesn't *know* how to love any more, it's all a performance. It has to be.

SIDNEY (*Avoiding a direct reply*)   If you could understand it, there is a great compliment to you in how I treated this, Alt. The compliment I thought you would be man enough to absorb and help Gloria like you wanted to help the rest of the world once. (ALTON *just laughs*)

ALTON   Talk to me man to man today, Sidney: Would you marry her?

SIDNEY   Alton, for Christ's sake! You were a revolutionary! Doesn't that stand for anything any more? It is one thing to take bread to the Bowery and another to eat it with them!

ALTON   *Would you marry her?*

SIDNEY   If I loved her . . . I don't know how to say it to you except that if I loved her . . .

ALTON (*Screaming*)   Don't you know some of the things these girls have to do?

SIDNEY   All right, I know. You are afire with all the images; every faceless man in the universe has become—

ALTON   Someone who has coupled with my love . . . used her like . . . an . . . inanimate object . . . a thing, an instrument . . . a commodity . . .

SIDNEY (*With supreme compassion for all*)   In an effort to assuage something of his own pathetic needs, Alton . . .

ALTON   A commodity! (*Looking up at* SIDNEY) Don't you understand, Sidney? (*Rubbing his head*) Man, like I am spawned from commodities . . . and their purchasers. Don't you *know* this? I am running from being a commodity. How do you think I got the color I am, Sidney? Haven't you ever thought about it? I got this color from my grandmother being used as a commodity, man. The buying and the selling in this country began with *me*. Jesus, help me.

SIDNEY   All right.

ALTON   You don't understand . . . My father, you know, he was a railroad porter . . . who wiped up spit and semen, carried drinks and white man's secrets for thirty years . . . When the bell rang in the night he put on that white coat and his smile and went shuffling through the corridors with his tray and whisk broom . . . his paper bags and his smile to wherever the white men were ringing . . . for thirty years. And my mother . . . she was a domestic. She always had, Mama did . . . bits of this and bits of that from the pantry of "Miss Lady," you know . . . some given, some stolen . . . And she would always bring this booty home and sit it all out on the kitchen table . . . So's we could all look at it . . . And my father . . . all the time he would stand there and look at it and walk away. And then one night, he had some kind of fit, and he just reached out and knocked all that stuff, the jelly, and the piece of ham; the broken lamp and the sweater for me and the two little vases . . . He just knocked it all on the floor and stood there screaming with the tears running down his face . . . "I ain't going to have the white man's leavings in my house, no mo'! I ain't going to have his *throw-away* . . . no mo'! . . ." And Mama, she just stood there with her lips pursed together and when he went to bed she just picked it all up, whatever hadn't been ruined or smashed, and washed it off and brushed it off and put it in the closet . . . and we *ate* it and *used* it . . . because we had to *survive,* and she didn't have room for my father's pride . . . I don't want white man's leavings, Sidney. I couldn't *marry* her. (*Getting up, and taking out a piece of paper*) I wrote her a note.

SIDNEY   Aren't you even going to see her? (ALTON *drops his head*) And if she was a black woman? (*It hangs*) That's racism, Alt.

ALTON   I know it—(*Touching his head*) here!

SIDNEY (*Sadly, looking at him*)   But—"A star has risen over Africa—"

ALTON (*Looking back at him*)   Yes.

SIDNEY   Over Harlem . . . over the South Side . . .

ALTON   Yes.

SIDNEY   The new Zionism is raging ... (ALTON *hands him the note, turns*) Aren't you even going to see her?

ALTON (*From the door, in anguish*)   No. I don't ever want to see her.
    (*He runs off.* SIDNEY *follows him out*)

SIDNEY   You are afraid that you would forgive her! And you don't want to do that, do you?
        (*Stands looking after him as the sounds of the victory celebration—not the song now, but the loudspeaker and crowd—envelop him. Presently* MAVIS *enters*)

MAVIS   Sidney Brustein!
        (*Arms outstretched, coming to him fast, sincerely impressed and overwhelmed. She steers him into the apartment, the closing door shuts out the sound*)

MAVIS   Who'd of ever thought it! First thing when Fred saw the paper this afternoon, he called me from the office and said, "Mav, that brother-in-law of yours is some kind of political genius!" He's so excited. Why, he said that everybody is talking about you and the paper and Wally O'Hara. He said that it even went out on the national news. (*She has hugged and kissed him through most of this*) Let's have a drink together, Sidney. I don't know how to tell you how proud I am. I just thought it was another one of those things that you are always doing—like with the night club—(*Correcting herself*) I know, it wasn't a night club—and all. Where is everyone? . . . I thought this place would be—you know—

SIDNEY (*Fixing her a drink*)   —"jumping." I wasn't the candidate, Mav. Iris hasn't come in yet. Sometimes she

103

stops off for the groceries . . . I'd like to entertain you, but I'm busy.

MAVIS   Groceries! Aren't you kids going out and celebrate? Honest to God, you're so strange— You don't even look happy.

SIDNEY   Oh, I'm happy . . . It's kind of freakish though, you know, that we won. We never dreamed we would. (*To himself, with wonder*) We never dreamed we would.

MAVIS   (*Takes a check out of her bag and puts it in* SIDNEY's *shirt pocket*)   Here's a little present, for the paper. (*Noting his astonishment*) From *Fred*, let's say. No, don't talk about it. Don't say a word. There it is. That's all.

SIDNEY   (*Looking at it*)   This is a *lot* of money, honey.

MAVIS   (*Drinking*)   I said let's not mention it and I mean it. When I—that is when *Fred*—decided that he would give it to you we agreed that we didn't want any chance whatsoever to feel good and gooey and Real Big about it. So— put it away.

SIDNEY   (*Looking at her, touched*)   Well, thank—you— (*With great ostentation, this error*) Oh, I mean, *Fred* for it.

MAVIS   (*Warmly*)   Shut up. (*Looking at him, the liquor warming and freeing her*) I'm glad to have a chance to talk with you, Sidney. Alone. We've never really talked— I know that you don't like me—

SIDNEY   (*Because that remark must embarrass anyone*) Mavis—

MAVIS   No, it's all right. I know it. You know it. When you come down to it, what is there to like? Isn't it funny how different sisters can be?

SIDNEY   Yes, different. All of us. Everything.

MAVIS   Yeeesss, don't I know it. I was trying to explain that to Fred the other day. (*A little laugh*) I don't mean I was trying to "explain" it . . . That sounds so funny: Fred isn't a stupid man, as we all know—but sometimes. Sometimes I get to thinking that certain kind of way. The way, you know, that *you* do— (*With her hands, a circle, and aptly, the universe*) of a whole—

SIDNEY   In abstractions.

MAVIS   That's right. ~~You won't believe it—but—I~~ enjoy it ~~when a person can say something so that it embraces~~ a lot, ~~so that it's in—in—~~

SIDNEY (*Staring at her*)   Concepts.

MAVIS   Yes. ~~I enjoy it.~~ I've enjoyed the conversations I've heard down here. And, Sidney, I've understood some of them.
    (*There is a curious, believable and quite charming defiance in this announcement*)

SIDNEY   Good for you, Mavis. Good for you.

MAVIS (*Oddly*)   But we get stuck, you know.

SIDNEY   Hmmm?

MAVIS   Some of us, we get stuck, in—(*Stiltedly*) the original stimuli. Some of us never have a chance, you know—

SIDNEY (*Nodding wearily, not wishing to hear this saga again*) I know—

MAVIS Like Papa—he was such a dreamer. You know, sort of backwoods poet, kind of a cross between Willy Loman and Daniel Boone. He loved just sitting and thinking—

SIDNEY (*Looking at her, stunned*) Didn't you and Iris have the same father?

MAVIS Of course we had the same father! What do you think I'm talking about?

SIDNEY *Rashomon*—what else?

MAVIS He was a very wonderful man, very wonderful. And that's the joke on me—I thought, I thought I was marrying someone like Papa when I married Fred. Can you imagine—*Fred!*

SIDNEY You mean you *wanted* him to be like your father?

MAVIS Yes . . . and that's the way I thought Fred was, in those days. He *seemed* poetic—when he was young. Do you know that Fred used to drive in forty miles from Ellensville to see me when we were courting? Forty miles and then back forty, and in the world's worst car. That's what he was like then. Like Papa. (*A little high*) Papa used to read the classics to us, you know, Greek tragedy. Sometimes in Greek.

SIDNEY (*Wide-eyed*) You are pulling my leg.

MAVIS (*Surprised*) Why? Oh, he didn't really know *classical* Greek, Sidney. Just everyday Greek from his folks, but that made it interesting . . . we used to do little productions in our living room. He would always let me be

Medea, because he said I was strong—(*She rises and bellows forth in robust, dramatic and effective Greek the following, enriching it with not badly conceived if stagey classical stance and gesture*) ʼΟ πόνος μέ περικυκλώνει ἀπό ὅλες τίς μεριές καί ποιός μπορεῖ νά τό ἀμφισβητήση. ʼΑλλά δέν χάθηκαν ἀκόμα ὅλα. Νομίζω ὄχι. (*Then in English, the first line or so, rather rattled off*) "On all sides sorrow pens me in. Who can gainsay this? But all is not yet lost! Think *not* so. Still there are troubles in store for the new bride and for her bridegroom—" Well, *he* thought I was good.

SIDNEY   Mavis, I don't know you.

MAVIS   The ham part, I know. (*A little laugh*) I know all the parts—and all the strophes. Sure, Papa was something! He was a man of great, great imagination. That's why he changed our name. It was plain old everyday Parodopoulos, you know—

SIDNEY   No, I didn't know.

MAVIS   But Papa wanted something, you know, *symbolic.* So he changed it to Parodus. You know what the parodus is in the development of Greek tragedy.

SIDNEY   Ah . . . no.

MAVIS   (*Proudly*)   Sidney! Shame on you! The parodus is the chorus! And you know—no matter what is happening in the main action of the play—the chorus is always there, commenting, watching. He said that we were like that, the family, at the edge of life—not changing anything. Just watching and being.

SIDNEY   (*Struck*)   I see.

MAVIS That was Papa, dramatic as hell. (*Drinking her drink*) I loved him very much. (*A beat*) And Fred's no Papa.

SIDNEY It's been one big disappointment, your marriage?

MAVIS (*Dully*) Not for a minute. I knew by the time that Fred and I got married that he wasn't the Fred he seemed to be. I knew what I was marrying and I was right. Solid as a rock. Hah! (*Abruptly*) We haven't touched each other more than twice since little Harry was born and that's . . . oh, six years now, isn't it? Harry will be six next month.

SIDNEY Ah—by whose—

MAVIS —design? Who knows? It just happens. (*Waving her hand*) He doesn't suffer. He's got a girl.

SIDNEY (*Gutterally*) Fred?

MAVIS (*Looking at him*) Fred. (*Shaking her head*) Sometimes I think you kids down here believe your own notions of what the rest of the human race is like. There are no squares, Sidney. Believe me when I tell you, everybody is his own hipster. Sure, for years now. Same girl, I'll say that for old Fred. I've met her.

SIDNEY (*He would genuinely like to seem blasé but he can't; he is truly astonished*) You have—?

MAVIS (*All with bitter restraint*) Oh sure. I went there. He has her all set up. Nothing fancy; Fred's strictly a family man, he puts the main money in the main place, our Fred. But decent, you know, respectable building, family people —a nice place for a single girl—(*The ultimate bitterness*) with a kid. (*He absorbs this with a silent start but knows to say nothing*) He's just a year younger than Harry. I saw him too. (*Now she is crying;* SIDNEY *is helpless in the face of this*) You do find out. And I did the usual: I hired a sordid little man to find out for sure. He did. And so, one day, I did what a woman has to do: I went to see. Not the spooky thing, I didn't want to come in on them together or any of that junk. I know what a man and a woman do; I just wanted to meet her. So I got in a cab, got out, rang a bell and there she was. Nothing like expected! Not a chorine or something as you always think, even with Fred, in my mind I had decided it would be some cheap mess; but no, there's this sandy-haired kid standing in pedal pushers and an apron, pregnant as all get-out. So I went in and we talked. And I went back, once, several months later—to see the baby. I had to see the baby. I didn't tell Fred about my knowing until after I saw the baby. And then, after that we went through the usual waltz . . . Divorce talk, all of it, you know.

SIDNEY   And then you decided against it.

MAVIS   Of course I decided against it. A divorce? For what? Because a marriage was violated? Ha! We've got three boys and their father is devoted to them; I guess he's devoted to all four of his boys. And what would I do? There was no rush years ago at home to marry Mavis Parodus; there was *just* Fred *then*. In this world there are two kinds of loneliness and it is given to each of us to pick. I picked. And, let's face it, *I* cannot type.

SIDNEY   (*Quietly shaking his head*)   But you want only simple people and simple problems in literature . . .

MAVIS Sure, isn't life enough?

SIDNEY Does Iris know any of this?

MAVIS What would I tell her for? Listen, we all play our roles. (*Long beat*) Well, one thing is sure. I do not need another drop to drink. (*Fixing herself, compact in hand*) So how is my cream-colored brother-in-law-to-be?

SIDNEY He's not going to be.

MAVIS Well, thank God for something. She broke it off, huh?

SIDNEY (*Looking up, absorbing the assumption*) Yes . . . I guess so.

MAVIS (*Blithe ignorance again*) It had to be. Look, the world's not ready. It just isn't. He seemed like a nice boy and all that, but it's just not possible. I mean in this world, you know. You have to think about children, you know. I knew Gloria would snap out of it. Why would she want to get into something like that? I mean he's very light, but— (*Halting*) I'm not fooling you, am I?

SIDNEY No.

MAVIS I can't help it, Sid. It's the way I feel. You can't expect people to change that fast.
    (*She gets up to go*)

SIDNEY (*Gently, more with wonder than assertion*) Mavis, the world is about to crack right down the middle. We've gotta change—or fall in the crack.

MAVIS (*Not angrily*) Well, I think we are back to ourselves and you are probably starting to insult me again. I knew I was going to tell you about it though, Sid—one of these days. I always knew that. Since I first saw you I knew those eyes could find a place for anybody's tale. Don't talk to Iris about it . . . I know I don't have to ask it of you, but all the same. Don't, huh? She's a kid, Sidney. She doesn't know what she's all about yet. She will, she'll get herself together one of these days. (*Patting his cheek*) And so will you. (*Looking at him*) Gee, we're proud of you, Sid. I told Fred, "Say what you will, but the Jews have get-up!"

SIDNEY (*In that kind of mood*)   Say what you will.

MAVIS   Now, there was nothing wrong with that, was there?

SIDNEY (*Smiling*)   Well, let's say there isn't. Today. (*A beat. She opens the door and we hear again the sounds of the rally*) Mavis, what do you do . . . I mean . . . ?

MAVIS   To make up for Fred, you mean? (*As he follows her out, by the stairs*) I take care of my boys. I shop and I worry about my sisters. It's a life.

SIDNEY (*A beat. Gently, lifting his fists to the gods above; it is for their ears only*)   "Witness you ever-burning lights above!" (*Then to her*) You're tough, Mavis Parodus. (*Kisses her—and, because she does have depth, MAVIS says nothing at all as she walks off. SIDNEY goes back in, pours a drink and stands looking out his window at the celebration. After a while IRIS enters. She looks completely different: she has been costumed somewhere in those precincts of the city where expressions of the couturier's need for yearly change of radical fashion are most evident. Her hair has been cut and teased to a stiff sculpture and tinted an entirely unnatural metallic yellow. She carries two shopping bags. SIDNEY is at the window and does not immediately see her*)

IRIS   Well, congratulations, Sid.

SIDNEY   Your sister was here.

IRIS   Oh? Which one?

SIDNEY   What do you mean, which one?

IRIS   Gloria is due. I didn't get a chance to tell you, but she is in town and she's coming by tonight.
(IRIS *goes into the bedroom*)

SIDNEY   Oh, my God, that's all I need.

IRIS   Since when aren't you glad to see Gloria?

SIDNEY   I'm always glad to see Gloria . . . Oh, never mind.

IRIS   (*Emerges with a traveling case*)   What did Mavis want?

SIDNEY   Nothing. Just to talk. We talked.
(*He turns and rather freezes at the change in her, but not for comedy*)

IRIS   I know. It looks pretty different. I won't ask if you like it. (*He is speechless and says nothing at all, merely stares as if he never really has seen her before. Brazening it out*) I got the job. Just like that—(*A snap*) they send you out to get fixed. (*She is putting on a new pair of shoes*) Everything but the shoes. They say it's gauche to walk out of a store in a pair of shoes you've just bought. At least that's what poor people say. I guess nothing is gauche if you're rich enough. (*Wise afterthought*) *Long* enough. Please don't stare at me like that, Sid. And let's don't discuss it.

SIDNEY   (*With thoughtfulness*)   Why did you always tell me all those stories about your father, Iris?

IRIS (*Looking up*)   You and Mavis had yourselves a real little old heart-to-heart, didn't you? What's the world coming to?

SIDNEY   Why did you make him out to be some kind of dull-witted nothing? What was the point of it?

IRIS (*Irritably, swiftly, falsely*)   Oh, why do you believe Mavis? She has some kind of transference about Papa. It's very complicated. When she talks about Papa she's really talking about this uncle of ours who—

SIDNEY (*Knowing that she is going into a long involved lie*) Never mind, Iris. It doesn't matter.

IRIS (*Sincerely*)   I guess—I just tried to live up to your fantasy about me. All of it. People do that —

SIDNEY   Let's not talk about that—

IRIS   You did a terrific job on the election. You must feel good.

SIDNEY (*Vaguely*)   Yes, I feel good. (*A beat*) Mavis said she thought we'd be going out to celebrate. You haven't told her anything then?

IRIS   No . . . who wants to hear all the wailing?

SIDNEY (*Looking at her, slowly, with emphasis*)   I have a feeling she'd survive it.

IRIS   Mavis' idea of marriage is something you do at twenty —and it stays that way—*no matter what*. Everything else shocks.

SIDNEY   Sure. Dullsville. (*Several beats; as he studies her and the things she has brought in*) What do you do? On the—(*Gestures "television"*) thing. I don't even know

113

what the hell it is that you're actually—(*He holds this word for a fraction longer than ordinary meaning would dictate. She has not missed this and so signifies by a lift of brow without, however, comment*) selling.

IRIS   Home permanents.

SIDNEY   (*Random gesture, not entirely innocent, circular waving of the hand*)   Is that what—uh—they've used on you?

IRIS   (*Determined not to let him provoke her*)   Don't be funny. This head has been in and out of all the booths in Mr. Lionel's for the last two and one half hours.

SIDNEY   But that's not what you are going to tell the people, is it? I mean you're not going to tell them that you got your —(*He looks at the box label*) Golden Girl Curl by sitting in Mr. Lionel's for several hours, are you?

IRIS   No, Sid, that certainly is not what I am going to tell them. I am going—(*Getting up and advancing on the Golden Curl sample*) to tell all the little housewifies that I just rolled it up on Golden Girl Curl . . . (*Before us, she assumes the manner of TV mannequins, holding up the box*) and rollers, using my magic Golden Girl Curl Box to hold everything just so . . . which you understand, is one of the main features of Golden Girl Curl Home Permanent.

SIDNEY   The box it comes in.

IRIS   (*With genuine loathing for the whole nonsense, enunciating with contempt*)   Yes! the box it comes in! (*She opens it—the bottom falls out and so do the rollers. Hurling it to the floor*) Which also does not work. (*Wheeling, crying, shrieking*) It's a job, Sidney! They do not pay you one hundred dollars an hour for hauling hamburgers at Hamlines. They do pay it for pretending that there is some difference between Golden Girl Curl and Wonder Curl, or between Wonder Curl and Home Perma Pearl, so what the hell do you want from me!

SIDNEY It doesn't work ...

IRIS (*Precisely now in the manner of a defensive child*) It does work. It does work enough to justify it. They just send you to the hairdressers to play safe. They have to have everything just so when they tape things for television, Sidney. You don't realize how expensive it is to tape something. All those lights and cameras and technicians . . . they can't have your hair falling down from some . . . (*Swiping at Golden Girl Curl again*) crappy old home permanent just when they're ready to shoot . . .

SIDNEY (*Getting up and going to her and taking her in his arms*) What's the matter, baby, what's happening to you? What's it all about—? What is it you're going after now? What is it that's got you all turned around? Where do you think it's heading you?

IRIS (*In his arms entirely, sobbing out rapidly and incoherently virtually all of the irrelevant parts of her problem*) Nothing . . . will put a curl in your hair . . . like this but . . . heat . . . But it works *some*, Sid, I did try it . . . Do you think the FTC would let them just put anything . . . on the air . . . like that . . . ?

SIDNEY Baby—

IRIS (*Shrieking—as the old comforting relationship threatens again*) I don't want to play Appalachian any more!

SIDNEY   All right, honey, but there's no reason to get all tied up in new games . . . Iris . . .

IRIS (*Shaking her head violently*)   You don't understand, you still don't understand. I am not the same . . . I am different . . .

SIDNEY (*Laughing, with wonder*)   Dear, sweet God . . . I've been living with a little girl . . . Iris, you really *are* a child.

IRIS (*Raising her face at that*)   Sidney . . . *One* of us here is a child and it's not me . . . I've found out plenty about the world in the last few weeks, and it's nothing like you—or Papa—want it to be . . . It's not! It's not . . . There are things talked about . . . laughed about while you stand there framed by that sign . . . that make me wonder how I ever thought you knew anything about this world at all . . . *This* world, Sidney! It's so dirty.

SIDNEY (*Rising now and crossing to her again*)   And what I am trying to tell you, little girl, is that you are learning the cynicism bit at the wrong time in our lives . . . (*He is gesturing toward the sign in the window. The crowd outside is heard again, muffled cheers and the Campaign Song*) We *won* something today, Iris. Not too much . . . just a little tiny part of the world turned right side up . . . Just listen . . .

IRIS (*The final outpouring*)   *Sidney! Stop it! I can't stand it ! ! !* You haven't won anything, Sid, they're all the same people! (*The revelation does not penetrate*) Don't you hear me? I tried to tell you . . . They *own* Wally . . . The people you've been fighting . . . Own him completely: the house he lives in, the clothes on his back, the toothpaste he uses. *They own* him, utterly, completely, entirely . . . (*Dragging him to the window*) There it is, Sid, the real world! Do you hear it? The world you say was just turned right side up!

(*A helpless hysterical gesture of flinging it at him*)

SIDNEY (*Frantically, shaking his head "no"—but his eyes saying "yes"*) What kind of psychotic filth is this?

IRIS It is filth. You don't know what filth, you can't *imagine* what filth! But it's not psychotic. Oh, Jesus, it's not even obscure . . . I have met people who didn't *believe* that you didn't know this . . . Jesus, Sid! I tried to tell you. Look, you can count on it, in a few months he'll be having press conferences to explain how the pinkos and the bohemians duped him in the first place and how he has found his way back to the "tried and true leadership" of the . . . "mother party"! (*She starts out, walking very much like the dead, picking up her bags. As she opens the door, the triumphant sounds of the crowd fill the room*) I would stay with you awhile now . . . if it would help anything. But it wouldn't. (*Turning, weeping freely*) I'll send for my things some time this week. Tell Gloria I'll phone her later. (*Then, suddenly*) For God's sake, Sidney, take down that sign! *It's like spit in your face!*

(*She exits. He reaches up and clutches the sign for a long moment, the tension mounting within him— but then releases it. Very much like a blind man, he moves to the drawing board, where his hand takes up the yardstick—the "sword of his ancestors"— which he holds aloft before him, saluting a foe that cannot be cut down . . . then lets it slip through his fingers. The sign pulses with a life of its own; the roar of the crowd grows louder; SIDNEY snaps the yardstick in half*)

Curtain

Act Three

Scene One

Time: Several hours later.

At rise: There is darkened gloom and quiet in the room and the place is a mess. SIDNEY *is stretched out under the coffee table, in considerable pain; one hand clutches at a center spot in his lower chest. An open whiskey bottle and glass are near. For some reason or other, in rough spasms, he harshly hums an old Yiddish melody,* "Rozhankis Mit Mandlen."

Presently, his sister-in-law GLORIA *appears at the door, carrying a small valise. She is about 26, as lovely as we have heard, but with surprising, fresh-faced, wholesome, "all-American" looks. She has a gleaming, casual, almost collegiate long bob, and the clothes are of that kind of lively smartness rather than dark elegance. With her valise she reminds one of a coed home for the weekend and no other thing. She knocks at the door; finally tries it and comes in.*

GLORIA (*Quizzically looking about in the shadows*)   Sidney? Sidney?
  (*She turns on a lamp*)

SIDNEY (*Roaring drunk, as it were*)   Stop it . . . Let there be darkness . . . Let the tides of night fall upon us and envelop us and protect us from the light . . . Shut it out, shut out the light . . . How do you like *them* apples, Goethe, old baby? Let there be darkness, I say! Out, I say! (*Then, recognizing her*) Gloria!

121

GLORIA   You're a nut!

SIDNEY   Gloria! (*She picks him up—drags him to couch*)

SIDNEY (*Singing "The Fireship" in reply: it is a song about a prostitute*)
>   "She had a bright and roving eye-eye!
>   And her hair hung down in ring-el-ets!"
>   (*He folds over and rather gags with pain*)
>   "A nice girl, a proper girl, but one
>   of the roving kind!"

GLORIA   You're having an attack—aren't you?
>   (*Thinks of it, then crosses to the refrigerator and gets a container of milk*)

SIDNEY   I'm all right!
>   (*Sings from the prone position*)
>   "Her hair hung down in ring-el-ets!"
>   (*Sitting up suddenly*)
>   No, that's not the one.
>   (*Lifts his head like a howling dog and sings starkly "Come All Ye Fair and Tender Ladies"*)
>   "If I'da known before I started
>   I never would have courted none
>   I'da locked my heart in a box of golden
>   and fastened it up with a silver pin."

GLORIA (*Offering the milk*)   Come on, Sidney, you're not all that drunk. C'mon, drink this.

SIDNEY (*Drinks, expecting liquor—spits out the milk*)
>   "Oh don't you remember the days of our courtin'
>   When your head lay upon my breast—"

GLORIA   What's going on, Sidney?

SIDNEY (*Opening his eyes*)   Can it be that the fall of man
has entirely escaped even *your* notice?

GLORIA   What do you mean?

SIDNEY   All—all that sweat; all that up-all-night; all that,
you should excuse the allusion— (*Hissing out the word*)
Passion. All for a mere flunky of Power. (*Gaily*) Who
cares anyhow? The world likes itself just fine the way it
is, so don't pick at it. That's all you gotta know about anything: Don't pick at it! (*He has crossed on these lines to
the door; he opens it and bellows up*) Hey, Hermes, come
on down: I'm ready to cross over the Styx. (*He turns
around and mugs heavily at* GLORIA) Get it: I'm just
going to hell with myself!
        (*He slaps his thigh burlesquing that kind of humor
        thickly*)

GLORIA   You need looking after. Where's Iris?

SIDNEY   Who? Oh, Iris. My wife. Who the hell knows.
(*Wandering around*) She was one of the lesser goddesses
anyhow. A kind of "girl Friday for Zeus," as they put it in
Time magazine. (*Posing*) Lookit me, who am I? (*Stands
on the couch—in Zeus pose;* GLORIA *can only laugh now*)
Come on, who am I? I'll give you a hint: I'm not Apollo.
In fact, I am not a god. (*As Jimmy Durante would say it*)
Ignore my stately bearing for the time being and look in
my eyes, and you will see there unmistakable—mortality.
(*Collapses again*) Here I am, Modern Man: flat on my
back with an oozing intestine, a bit of a tear frozen in the
corner of my eye, a glass of booze which will saturate
without alleviating . . . and not the dimmest notion of

123

what it is all about. (*He drinks and sits up*) And my wife has run off to capture lightning bolts for Zeus. On account of he pays well and you get to meet all the up and coming young gods and things.

DAVID (*Entering, coolly*) Well, I see I have entered in a large moment.

SIDNEY David, my boy! (*Throws the bottle*) The only man I happen to know personally who is unafraid of the dark. Have a drink.

DAVID You're drunk and silly and I have a guest.
(*He starts out*)

SIDNEY Well, bring her—excuse me—him down and we'll have a happening or something.

DAVID We're already having one, thank you.

SIDNEY (*Grabbing hold of him*) All that motion, all that urgency . . . for nothing. That's the whole show, isn't it? A great plain where neither the wind blows, nor the rain falls, nor anything else happens. *Really happens,* I mean. Besides our arriving there and one day leaving again . . . That's what your plays are about, aren't they?

DAVID Yes, I suppose so.

SIDNEY Billy said it better than you though: ". . . a tale told by an idiot, full of sound and fury, signifying nothing." Billy said everything better.

DAVID I won't argue. What's happened?

SIDNEY Nothing . . . everything . . . And I won't argue with you any more either, David. You're right about everything.

DAVID Well, at least you are learning.

SIDNEY Oh yes, and to laugh! Finally. At the colossal absurdity. It's the only refuge, the only cove of endurance. To accept it all and offer back only a cold . . . shadowless stream of laughter. (*Does a vaudeville turn and strikes another especially ludicrous pose. Sings*)
  "Oh, we're lost—out here in the stars!"
(*Turning, as if seeing her for the first time*) Gloria!
  (*He holds out his arms to her. She goes to him and they embrace; there is a quite genuine affection between these two. He holds her rather desperately, and inadvertently, hurts her*)

SIDNEY What's the matter?

GLORIA (*Covering quickly*) Some bruises. It's all right. Are *you* all right?
  (SIDNEY *grabs his mouth; starts for the bathroom with great dignity which he cannot sustain; he breaks and runs in, closing door behind him. She notes* DAVID *fully for the first time*)

GLORIA And you must be—

DAVID David Ragin. Hi.

GLORIA (*With recognition*) From upstairs. Hi. I'm—

DAVID Gloria. The sister who—"travels a lot." (*As she clearly reacts to his emphasis*) Oh, it's all right. I practically live here and it's, like, all in the family, no secrets. I do naughty things with boys only—so relax.

GLORIA You're very free with personal information.

DAVID (*Blithely*) Isn't it the great tradition for writers and whores to share the world's truths?

GLORIA (*Spinning with astonishment and fury*) Listen, I don't like your language—or you.

DAVID I'm sorry. I didn't know it would upset you.

GLORIA Weren't you leaving?

DAVID I said I was sorry. And I almost never apologize to anyone. I apologized to you—because I respect you.

GLORIA I said, weren't you leaving?

DAVID Look—it's okay with me. Relax. I'm writing about a—girl—like you. I cut away all the hypoc—

GLORIA Look, little boy—(*Sudden strong, throaty tones*) I've never met you before, but I have met them like you a hundred times and I know everything you are about to say; because it's been asked and written four thousand times . . . anything I would tell you, you would believe it and put it down and feel like you'd been close to something old and deep and wise. Any bunch of lies I would make up. Well, these are not office hours. Now get the hell out of here!
    (*Rising, she winces and catches her side*)

DAVID What's hurting you?

GLORIA (*In apparent physical pain*) Please be some kind of gentleman if you—think you can *swing* it and go away.

DAVID (*Looking at her hard*) You really don't like your life?!

GLORIA (*Her head back, her eyes closed*) The things people think in this world—!

DAVID   Can I get you something?

GLORIA   Just go away!
(*He exits.* SIDNEY *re-enters, his head—and shirt— doused with water, affecting sobriety, to little avail. He looks a state, crosses to* GLORIA *at the bar, carrying one shoe*)

SIDNEY (*At the bottle*)   Want a drink? Oh, I always forget —about you and your face, the tissues and all.

GLORIA   It's all right—I'm learning to like it. (*Slapping playfully at the underchin and cheeks*) Let the damn tissues fall! (*Looking up at him, softly*) I've quit, Sid. *Really* quit.

SIDNEY (*Changing the subject*)   How did you—hurt your-self?

GLORIA   I didn't. That's the result of an evening spent with six and one half feet of psycho. I happen to have a predi— What do you call it?

SIDNEY   Predilection?

GLORIA   Predilection for psychos and vice cops, it's quite amazing! To the point where some of the girls tease me about it. This last one . . . I think he was trying to kill me. It was his thing . . . you know, violence. (*Looking around*) When's Iris coming? She must be working hard, this place is a wreck!

SIDNEY   She'll be along.

GLORIA (*Grinning*)   Hey—Sid, lookit me! (*Holding up the glass triumphantly*) Whiskey. I've joined the human race. No more goofball pills—I'm kicking everything. (*She makes a comic face and their glasses clink*) I did the whole gooey farewell bit with some of the kids. Adios, Muchachas! I'm going to marry him. Yes, I mean *after* we talk about it. I wouldn't unless I told him. I know girls who've done that. Doesn't work out. Never works out. You run into people. They make up all kinds of nutty things, but it doesn't work out. I'm going to sit down and say—(*A swinging recitation brimming over with confidence to conceal terror below: rehearsed too many times to perfection because she knows it won't work. The voice is bright with an assurance the eyes deny*) "I was a nineteen-year-old package of fluff from Trenersville, Nowhere, and I met this nothing who took one look at this baby face of mine and said, 'Honey, there's a whole special market for you. Slink is on the way out; all-American wholesomeness is the rage. You've got it made! You'll be part of the aristocracy of the profession!' Which is true. Only it's the profession they don't exactly describe. After that you develop your own rationales to make it all right to yourself: a) It's old as time anyhow; (*They clink glasses loudly and laugh*) b) (*Hand on heart—for God and country*) It's a service to society; (*They clink again*) and c) The *real* prostitutes are everybody else; especially housewives and career girls. (*Again they howl*) We trade those gems back and forth for hours. Nobody believes it, but it helps on the bad days. And, sweetie, there are a lot of bad days.

SIDNEY   Gloria—no matter what happens, honey, you've got to stick to that.

GLORIA   (*Glass poised in midair, she lowers it slowly*)

Okay, Sid, what is it—a letter or a phonograph record with violins?

SIDNEY Gloria—

GLORIA (*Supreme effort at self-control: to both steel herself for—and hold off—the inevitable*) I was on this date once, Sid. He had a book of reproductions by Goya. And there was this one—an etching, I think. Have you ever seen it? There's this woman, a Spanish peasant woman and she's standing like this—reaching out. And what she's reaching for are the teeth of a dead man. A man who'd been hanged. And she is rigid with—revulsion, but she wants his teeth, because it said in the book that in those days people thought that the teeth of the dead were good luck. Can you imagine that? The things people think they have to do? To *survive*? Some day I'm going to buy that print. It's all about my life . . .

SIDNEY He loves you, honey. He loves you terribly . . .

GLORIA (*Tough, hoarse urgency: she is ready for it now*) Come on, Sidney! (SIDNEY *hands her the letter. There is presently in the silence only the single hurt outcry of any small creature of the forest, mortally struck. She crumples the letter in her hand. He crosses to her swiftly, tries to comfort her in his arms; she throws back a girlish head and emits now a cry deep, guttural and as primeval as the forest*) Men! Oh God, men!

SIDNEY (*Pouring a drink fast and trying to push it on her*) Come on—drink this for me—

GLORIA Get that trash out of my face, Sidney. Get it away —(*She knocks it away and rises; he tries to block this, but the inner sense of futility makes it a half-hearted*

129

effort) Where's my handbag! Get out of my way, Sidney. Come on, who needs this world the way it is! (*Pulling free with a mighty jerk*) Let go! (*She gets the bag and downs the pills, calming long before the effect, simply because she knows that they are inside*) You see, no fuss, no muss ... Drugs are the coming thing, Sid. Do you keep up with all the writings on mescalin and all? I find it fascinating ... (*She lies down on the sofa. Her reversion is progressive; she is pushing hard for it; not letting the pills do it. Now she is drinking also*) Ha—you want to hear something! I was going to marry that vanilla dinge! Do you know what some of the other girls do—they go off and they sleep with a colored boy—and I mean *any* colored boy so long as he is black—because they figure that is the one bastard who can't look down on them five seconds after it's over! And I was going to *marry* one!

SIDNEY (*Crossing to* GLORIA) Maybe he'll change his mind. He was sort of in a state of shock about it. I mean, try to understand, it's very complicated about Alton—

GLORIA Oh, so *he's* in a state of shock! Oh Jesus, that yellow-faced bastard! *He's* shocked. Look, Sid, I'll bet you two to one that at this instant he is lying dead drunk in the arms of the blondest or blackest two-bit hooker in town. *Nursing* his shock! Telling his tale of woe! *His* tale! She'll be telling it somewhere by morning to the girls and roaring with laughter ... Like I'm doing. Aw, what the hell am I carrying on for—it wouldn't have worked. And besides, the life beats the hell out of that nine-to-five jazz. (*Suddenly a violent sob*) Sidney! What happened to my life! (*He tries to go to her; she holds out a hand to stay him*) I'll be twenty-six this winter and I have tried to kill myself three times since I was twenty-three . . . I was always awkward . . . But I'll make it. Or maybe a looney trick will be thorough some night. (*Sitting up*) Well . . . that's enough gloom and doom, everybody! Come on, Sidney brother, cheer up. (*She rumples his hair, nuzzles playfully in a desperate effort at gaiety and release*) After all, how many things could a nice normal healthy American girl kick all at one time—the racket and the pills? And take on integration, too? Tch! Tch! (*Weaving toward the phonograph*) Let's have some music. And none of that creepy stuff my creepy father used to play. (*She puts on a record—some very modern jazz; it throbs low and warm and intense*) Yeah . . . that's good. I have to have music . . . it helps to close things out. It envelops you. (*She beckons and* SIDNEY *moves into her arms; they begin to dance in a tight embrace, he in a bemused and delicious half-stupor; she as if, in the mere physical body contact, she were clinging to life. Now the denaturalization of these moments begins to heighten as per their state. A light, deathly blue, of great transparency, settles slowly and as imperceptibly as possible; it gives way to a hot and sensual fuchsia. The music follows suit—the more familiar jazz sounds going even beyond their own definitions. When each speaks it is stiffly and unnaturally, intoned with a heightened, fragmented assertion beyond sense or sequence, as if lucidity no longer required logic. An absurdist orgy is being created in front of us—a disintegration of reality to parallel the disintegration in* SIDNEY's *World*) Things as they are are as they are and have been and will be that way because they got that way because things were as they were in the first place.

(DAVID *re-enters; he has come downstairs slowly, glancing up the stairs and halting a couple of times. Now he stands just inside the door, watching* GLORIA *and* SIDNEY *as the heat mounts between them*)

SIDNEY   "Society is based on complicity in the common crime . . . We all suffer from the murder of the primal father who kept all the females for himself and drove the sons away. So we murdered him and, cannibals that we are, ate him."

DAVID   Sidney, you've finally joined the human race! Welcome to the club.

SIDNEY (*To* DAVID)   We are all guilty, therefore all guilt is equal. Therefore none are innocent, therefore—none are guilty. Any two of anything is totalitarian.
(SIDNEY *breaks away to lie down on the couch as* DAVID *crosses to take his place as* GLORIA's *dancing partner, melting into her outstretched arms*)

GLORIA   Whaddaya do if your own father calls you a tramp . . . on his deathbed . . . huh? Whaddaya do?

SIDNEY (*On his back, rousing, with a flourish*)   You only *think* that flowers are fragrant. 'Tis an illusion!

DAVID   Trying to live with your father's values can kill you. Ask me, I know.

GLORIA   No, sweetie, living *without* your father's values can kill you. Ask me, I know.

SIDNEY (*Sings*)
"Ohhhhhhhh—
This is the way the cheese will rot!

The cheese will rot! The cheese will rot!
Oh this is the way the cheese will rot!
All on a Sunday morning!"

DAVID   Any profession of concern with decency is the most indecent of all human affectations.

SIDNEY (*Rising suddenly with great vigor*)   To be or not to be! (*A great pause, he sears us with his eyes—then falls back*) Well, better leave *that* one alone!

SIDNEY, GLORIA *and* DAVID (*In disjointed unison*)
"Oh, who's afraid of Absurdity! Absurdity! Absurdity!
Who's afraid of Absurdity!
Not we, not we, not we!"
    (*As* SIDNEY *dozes off on the sofa,* GLORIA *stops* DAVID
    with a long wet kiss, then steps back, a little shaken)

DAVID (*As much disengaged from her as she is from him. With wistful melancholy*)   All your life you want certain things and when you try to trace them back with the finger of your mind to where you believe you first started to want them, there is nothing but a haze . . . I was seven. So was Nelson. We were both exactly seven. We used to make a great deal out of that. We used to play all day in my yard. He had fine golden hair and a thin delicate profile—(*He traces her mouth with the fingers of one hand, touches her hair*) and Mother always said: "Nelson is a real aristocrat." (*He crosses back to the table where she is staring off glassy-eyed*) Then, just like that, one summer his family moved to Florence, Italy. Because that is the sort of thing that aristocrats do when they feel like it. And I never saw him again.

GLORIA (*Nodding up and down drunkenly*) And you've been looking for him ever since.

DAVID He never came back.

GLORIA And now . . .

DAVID There is a beautiful burnished golden boy very much like Nelson sitting on a chair upstairs. He is from one of the oldest, finest families in New England. He is exquisite. But great damage has been done to him—

GLORIA (*For this girl there are no surprises left*) He requires . . . the presence of a woman . . . Not just any girl, but someone young enough, fresh enough, in certain light, to make him think it is somebody of his own class—

DAVID Yes. But—there is nothing to do. Apparently—it is merely a matter of—watching.

GLORIA (*Raising her eyes pathetically*) And *you're* a friend of Sidney's . . .

DAVID It's not for me. Perhaps you can understand: If he asked for the snows of the Himalayas tonight, I would try to get it for him. I thought—you might know of such things.

GLORIA (*Agonized*) Oh . . . I know of such things!

DAVID Will you come up—?

GLORIA (*A beat. Not really to him*) Sure . . . why not?

DAVID It's apartment three-F.

(*He goes out and up.* GLORIA *stands for a long moment, looking after him, then crosses quickly to the phonograph, which she turns up louder, as if to drown out some voice that speaks only to her, till the*

134

persistent lonely chaos of the music fills the room. She tries to dance a little, that doesn't work; she downs more goofball pills with liquor. Then, snapping her fingers and undulating a little to the rhythms in the room, with a fixed smile, she goes out. But as she mounts the third step, she freezes in the grip of a physical revulsion she can no longer contain—then suddenly whirls)

GLORIA *(Her words are a single guttural cry of pain)* Sick people belong in hospitals!!! *(For a long moment her eyes dart frantically and she whimpers, trapped, seeking refuge. There is none. At last she looks at the bottle of pills in her hand, walks slowly back and stands, spent, in the doorway. Then, resolutely:)* Papa—I **am** better than this! Now will you forgive me—?

(She crosses to the bathroom, clutching the bottle, halts, terrified at the unseen presence there, turns away; but then, with a final lift of her head, she enters and closes the door. The phone begins to ring as the lights slowly dim. SIDNEY *sleeps on)*

Dimout

Scene Two

Time: Early the next morning.

At rise: There is now a stark, businesslike and cold atmosphere in the apartment, as opposed to the tone of the last scene. It is just after dawn; in the course of this scene the blue-gray of the hour slowly lifts, until, at the end, the sun breaks full. A DETECTIVE, *with pad, routinely questions* IRIS, *who sits in the rocker facing front; slumped, in her coat, hands in pockets, eyes red and staring off at nothing in particular. For its part, the sign seems more naked now, more assertive, more dominating and, for all of its unnoticed presence, necessary. The bathroom door stands ajar.*

DETECTIVE   Age of the deceased?

IRIS   Twenty-six.

DETECTIVE   Your relationship?

IRIS   My sister.

DETECTIVE   Occupation? (SIDNEY *enters, in his coat, stands in the door for a moment, as if the mere fact of the apartment oppresses him.* IRIS *says nothing. The* DETECTIVE *coughs, tries again, anxious to get it over*) Occupation of the deceased?

SIDNEY   Like, she was a member of the chorus.

136

DETECTIVE   Chorus girl—?
>   (*He starts to write that;* IRIS *looks up but says nothing*)

SIDNEY   No—no, she was a model.

DETECTIVE (*Putting his book away*)   All right. You know there's gonna be an inquest.
>   (IRIS *offers no response.* SIDNEY *finally nods. The* DETECTIVE *exits*)

SIDNEY   I got them a cab. When they got home, Fred said, he'd call the doctor and have Mavis sedated. (*Paces agitatedly. Halting and looking at her*) You should let it come, honey . . . Cry. It's worse if you do what you're doing . . . (*He spots* GLORIA's *headband on the floor, where she had dropped it; he picks it up, stands looking at the bathroom, then turns away—with a face contorted— to face his wife. A long beat. Then helplessly*) You want a cup of tea or something? (IRIS *gives a quick, tight, little shake of her head "no."* WALLY *appears at the door, knocks, though it is ajar. He comes in, hat in hand, face cut with concern.* SIDNEY *just looks at him. A beat. Then grandly*) I see, Wally: the drama has come of age! The deus ex machina no longer comes floating in with its heavenly resolution—or dissolution—it merely comes walking through the door—*like a man.*

WALLY (*To* IRIS)   I heard about—your sister. (*Awkwardly, sincerely*) There's never anything to say, is there? But if there's anything I can do. (IRIS *does not respond in any way. To* SIDNEY *softly*) She's in bad shape, Sidney. Why don't you call a doctor?

SIDNEY (*With an effort at restraint*) What do you want here, Wally?

WALLY I know, Sidney, you think I'm the prince of all the bastards—

SIDNEY No, as a matter of fact, it's been my opinion for some time now that the merely ambitious have enjoyed too much stature through the centuries: I think you're a rather rank-and-file bastard.

WALLY (*With a half smile*) It feels *good*, doesn't it, Sid? It must feel good: to be able to judge! One good betrayal vindicates all our own crimes, doesn't it? Well, I'm going to tell you something I learned a long time ago—

SIDNEY (*Swiftly, angrily, as if by rote*) "If you want to survive you've got to swing the way the world swings!"

WALLY It's true. You either negotiate or get out of the race. Face up, Sid—or is that too hard for you?—that I'm the same man I was a year ago. Two months ago. Last week. And I still believe I am making my contribution to changing things—but I happen to know that in order to get anything done, anything at all in this world, baby, you've got to know where the power is. That's the way it's always been and that's the way it always will be.

SIDNEY How do you know?

WALLY (*As if there is no end to the innocence in this house*) Baby—I am *of* this world; it's something you know.

SIDNEY (*Fingering* GLORIA's *headband; a private irony*) And besides— (*Softly*) "all the *real* prostitutes are everybody else."

WALLY (*Ready for him*) Name calling is the last refuge of ineffectuals. You rage and I function. Study that some-times, Sid. (*Crossing to the window*) Look, you know that stop sign that the housewives have been trying to get at Macklin and Warren Streets? With the baby-carriage demonstrations and the petitions and all? Well, they'll get their stop sign now. *I'll* get it for them. But not as some wide-eyed reformer. And better garbage collection and the new playground and a lot of other things too.

SIDNEY (*Half smile*) And the narcotic traffic? What about that?'

WALLY (*A quick hand-waving*) That's more complicated. There's more involved. You don't go jumping into things.

SIDNEY (*Instinctively, swiftly*) I see: We can go on step-ping over the bodies of the junkies—but the trains will run on time!
(*He clicks his heels and throws off the Fascist salute smartly*)

WALLY (*Throwing his head back, just a little*) As a matter of fact, I knew it would be like this. That you would be standing there with that exact expression on your face, smoking a cigarette . . . filled with all the simple self-righteousness of bleeding innocence again betrayed. Well, I've got only this to say about it, Sid—

SIDNEY (*Suddenly, without warning—the confrontation. The real one*) *They're after my paper now, aren't they, Wally?*

WALLY (*Thrown; he would have preferred this on his own ground*) You don't understand. They don't want anything . . . Look, I told them not to expect to buy you, Sid. (*The latter smiles and nods his head throughout*) I've made them understand that . . . Nothing changes. You go on exactly as before, that's all.

SIDNEY   Ah! I see: you mean covering the art shows, doing charming little photographic essays of the snow on our quaint little streets.

WALLY   Yes!

SIDNEY   And leave the world—to you?

WALLY   I didn't do you in, Sid. You did yourself in and there ought to be a lesson in it for you: stay up in the mountains with your banjos and your books where you belong.

SIDNEY   But should I persist?

WALLY   Sidney, I am talking to you as a friend . . .

SIDNEY   *Should I persist?*

WALLY   (*Had not wanted to say it like this*)   Then the paper won't last six months.

SIDNEY   (*With wonder—genuine wonder*)   Wally, don't you know what kind of a house you've walked into? Didn't it hit you in the face? Didn't death breathe on you as you came through the door? What's the matter with you, man? While I lay stoned on that couch, a girl who tried to accept everything that you stand for died in that bathroom today. Do you think I haven't learned anything in the last few hours? The slogans of capitulation can *kill!* Every time we say "live and let live"—death triumphs!

WALLY   Sidney, what it is that you're trying to say?

SIDNEY   That I am going to fight you, Wally. That you
have forced me to take a position. Finally—the one thing
I never wanted to do. Just not being *for* you is not enough.
Since that girl died—(*To* IRIS) I'm sorry, honey, but I
have to—since that girl died—I have been forced to learn
I have to be *against* you. And, Wally, I am against you—
I swear it to you—and your machine. And what you have
to worry about is the fact that some of us will be back out
in those streets today. Only this time—thanks to you—we
shall be more seasoned, more cynical, tougher, harder to
fool—and therefore, less likely to quit.

WALLY (*The genuine passion of the compromised*)   Sidney,
you reek of innocence!

IRIS (*Suddenly, turning*)   The question is, Wally, what is
it *you* reek of?

SIDNEY (*To* WALLY, *but the words are intended for* IRIS)
I'll tell you what he reeks of: He reeks of accommodation.
He reeks of collusion. He reeks of collaboration—with
Power and the tools of Power . . . (*To* WALLY) Don't you
understand, man? Too much has happened to me! I love
my wife—I want her back. I loved my sister-in-law. I
want to see her alive. I—I love you—I should like to see
you redeemed. But in the context in which we presently
stand here I doubt any of this is possible. That which
warped and distorted all of us is—(*Suddenly lifting his
hands as if this were literally true*) all around; it is in this
very air! *This world*—this swirling, seething madness—
which you ask us to accept, to help maintain—has done
this . . . maimed my friends . . . emptied these rooms and
my very bed. And now it has taken my sister. *This* world!
Therefore, to live, to breathe—I shall *have* to fight it!

WALLY (*Picking up his hat—shaking his head*) That's asking for it, Sidney . . .

SIDNEY Then that should be the first thing I tell my readers —while I still can.

WALLY (*Gesturing incredulously to* IRIS, *as if to an ally*) Am I really supposed to believe this—? (IRIS *slowly nods "yes"—then shrugs with innocence: What can she do with* SIDNEY? WALLY *turns back with genuine wonder*) You really are a fool.

SIDNEY Always have been. (*His eyes find his wife's*) A fool who believes that death is waste and love is sweet and that the earth turns and men change every day and that rivers run and that people wanna be better than they are and that flowers smell good and that I hurt terribly today, and that hurt is desperation and desperation is—energy and energy can *move* things . . .

WALLY (*Looking from one to the other; pronounced exasperation with "children"*) Let me know the time and place of the funeral, won't you? I'd like to send flowers.
> (*He starts out, adjusts his hat, notes the sign, gazes at them and then wanders off.* IRIS *rises*)

IRIS For a long time now I've been wanting something. For a long time. I think it was for you to be all of yourself. I want to come home, Sidney. I want to come home but . . .

SIDNEY We'll talk about it.
> (*With a supreme mustering of will, and her whole body, she pushes shut the bathroom door, as if on the Past—and yet for a moment longer stands transfixed by it—then turns and crosses to* SIDNEY *on the couch*)

IRIS (*Holding her hands before her and turning them slowly*) When she was little . . . she had fat, pudgy hands . . . and I used to have to scrub them . . . because she couldn't get them clean. And so I would pretend that they were fish and I was the Fish Lady cleaning these little fish to sell them . . . That always tickled her so, and she would laugh and laugh and . . .

(*She gags on the first great sob, he folds her into his arms and, in the desperateness of this contact without words, the tears come freely now*)

SIDNEY Yes . . . weep now, darling, weep. Let us both weep. That is the first thing: to let ourselves feel again . . . Then, tomorrow, we shall make something strong of this sorrow . . . (*They sit spent, almost physically drained and motionless . . . as the clear light of morning gradually fills the room*)

Curtain